THE DOG IN THE MANGER

Lope de Vega
THE DOG IN THE MANGER
A new translation by David Johnston

OBERON BOOKS

LONDON

The Royal Shakespeare Company

The Royal Shakespeare Company is one of the world's best-known theatre ensembles, which aims to create outstanding theatre relevant to our times. The RSC is at the leading edge of classical theatre, with an international reputation for artistic excellence, accessibility and high quality live performance.

The Spanish Golden Age celebrates one of the most dynamic, energetic and stylish periods of world drama that is, astonishingly, hardly known to any of us. The four neglected plays from 17th century Spain which the RSC chose to present dramatised our fascination with the themes of seduction, honour and revenge. The season was unique in a number of ways. It was the first time that an ensemble of British actors had come together over a period of time to bring these plays to life. It is also a new venture for the RSC and importantly for many of our audience who will not have had the opportunity to see the plays before.

The RSC performs throughout the year at our home in Stratford-upon-Avon and that work is complemented by a presence in other areas of the UK. We play regularly in London and at an annual residency in Newcastle upon Tyne. In addition, our mobile auditorium tour sets up in community centres, sports halls and schools in areas throughout the UK with little access to professional theatre.

While the UK is the home of our Company, our audiences are global. We regularly play to theatregoers in other parts of Europe, across the United States, the Americas, Asia and Australasia and we are proud of our relationships with partnering organisations throughout the world.

The RSC is at heart an ensemble Company. The continuation of this great tradition informs the work of all members of the Company. Directors, actors, dramatists and theatre practitioners all collaborate in the creation of the RSC's distinctive and unmistakable approach to theatre.

 # The Royal Shakespeare Company

A PARTNERSHIP WITH THE RSC

The RSC relies on the active involvement and the direct charitable support of our audience members for contributions towards our work. Members of our audience also assist by introducing us to companies, foundations and other organisations with which they have an involvement – and help us demonstrate that in return for either philanthropic or sponsorship support, we can deliver benefit to audiences, local communities, school groups and all those who are given enhanced access to our work through private sector support.

RSC PATRONS AND SHAKESPEARE'S CIRCLE

Personal contributions from RSC Patrons provide essential financial support for our artists, educationalists and their students, young writers and audience members that require special access services.

For more information, please contact the Development Department on **01789 272283**.

CORPORATE PARTNERSHIPS

The RSC has a global reputation, undertaking more international touring each year than any other UK arts organisation. Our profile is high; our core values of artistic excellence and outstanding performance can be aligned with commercial values and objectives.

Our extensive range of productions and outreach and education programmes help ensure that we identify the best opportunity to deliver your particular business objectives. A prestigious programme of corporate hospitality and membership packages is also available.

For more information, please contact the Development Department on **01789 272283**.

For detailed information about opportunities to support the work of the RSC, visit **www.rsc.org.uk/support**

This production of *The Dog in the Manger* was first performed by the Royal Shakespeare Company in the Swan Theatre, Stratford-upon-Avon, on 14 April 2004.

The original cast was as follows:

Claire Cox	Marcela
Rebecca Johnson	Diana
Katherine Kelly	Clara
Melanie Machugh	Dorotea
Emma Pallant	Anarda
Joseph Chance	Fabio
Julius D'Silva	Celio
Joseph Millson	Teodoro
Oscar Pearce	Count Federico
John Ramm	Marquis Ricardo
Matt Ryan	Antonelo
Peter Sproule	Octavio
John Stahl	Ludovico
Simon Trinder	Tristan
John Wark	Furio
Oliver Williams	Lirano/Leonido/Camilo

Directed by	Laurence Boswell
Designed by	Es Devlin
Lighting designed by	Ben Ormerod
Music composed by	Ilona Sekacz
Sound designed by	Tim Oliver
Choreography by	Heather Habens
Fights directed by	Terry King
Assistant Director	Tom Daley
Music Director	Michael Tubbs
Voice and dialect work by	Jeannette Nelson
Casting Director	John Cannon CDG
Production Manager	Pete Griffin
Associate Costume Designer	Emma Williams

Company Manager	Jondon
Stage Manager	Paul Sawtell
Deputy Stage Manager	Zoe Donegan
Assistant Stage Manager	Jenny Grand

Contents

INTRODUCTION: Making Theatre Happen, 11

THE DOG IN THE MANGER, 23

First published in 2004 by Oberon Books Ltd
521 Caledonian Road, London N7 9RH
Tel: 020 7607 3637 / Fax: 020 7607 3629
info@oberonbooks.com
www.oberonbooks.com

A catalogue record for this book is available from the British Library.

ISBN: 978-1-84002-435-7

Cover Design: Anne-marie Comarsh, RSC Graphics
Photograph: Cristina Rodero / agence VU

Introduction

MAKING THEATRE HAPPEN

Félix Lope de Vega y Carpio was born in Madrid, on 25 November 1562, barely a few months before Philip II began the enormous undertaking of the construction of the monumental royal palace and pantheon of El Escorial in the foothills of the sierra, to the north west of the city. It was a building that in many ways symbolised the great Spanish imperial dream, funded by gold gouged from the New World, where Spain had relentlessly been extending its power since 1492. These were times of great expansion and of official optimism, culminating in the arrogant dubbing of the Armada of 1588 as 'invincible'. But, before that, chinks and then cracks had begun to open up inside the heart of empire itself. The picaresque novel had already begun to probe these fault-lines in the middle of the sixteenth century. With its cynical irony and its cold eye for the twisted, the jaundiced and the deformed, the picaresque raises angry questions about the rigidity of the moral and economic universe that had been passed down and conserved from Aristotelian teachings. Outside Spain, there was a stirring of ideas; traditionalist assumptions were subjected to a pressure of inquiry that stemmed from heresies and new religious doctrines, as well as from the nascent modern scientific scepticism marked by the spirit of Galileo's 'e pur si muove'. But in a country not long united against the Moors and Jews, there was always the fear of the enemy within, and speculative thought and competing understandings of reality were held forcefully at bay. The Inquisition drew up its indexes of prohibited books, as Spain closed down its intellectual frontiers.

It is frequently argued that censorship creates a censored mentality. There is no doubt that Lope de Vega, as he is more readily known, exercised a degree of self-censorship in his theatre. Lope's life was full of erotic incidents and relationships, and there is an erotic charge in his work that gives it its characteristic vital energy. More than anything else, Lope writes about love, perhaps not in the 'swarming, fanciful and excited' words of Shakespeare, as Borges describes them (in Di Giovanni's translation), but in a more restricted and formally-controlled language that moves explicitly within the horizon of expectations of an audience that encompassed all echelons of society, from poorly-paid workers right up to his own royal patron. This is not to say that he doesn't frequently test the limits of the permissive. His plays have many moments in which the shroud of social decorum is lifted momentarily to allow his audiences to sense the flood of this erotic energy, coursing like a river below, all the more forceful now for its uneasy containment – enough such moments, indeed, for a council of eminent theologians to recommend the banning of his theatre in 1646, just over a decade after his death.

Lope was, of course, a professional man of the theatre. His sense of the practical demands of performance is evident in many tiny details of his plays. He knew his audiences, and he also knew how to keep them engaged, with exciting excursions into the liminal, those dangerous spaces where desire threatens to destabilise the law, before reassuring them with final images of order restored. And his output was legendary, even in his own lifetime. If we accept even the lowest possible estimate of pieces attributed to him, Lope completed a new play, on average, every two months of the fifty-five years of his life as a writer. And that is to ignore all the other writings – religious autos, poetry, pastoral novels, and dramatic treatises – produced throughout a life lived generously and to the full.

In 1562, Madrid had recently become the country's capital, with the transfer to the city of Philip II's court from a series of medieval and renaissance capitals – Burgos, Valladolid and Toledo – whose strategic importance had declined since the Reconquest. The city suddenly found itself the hub of much of the known world, with a rapid influx of new inhabitants who, like Lope's own audiences, mirrored every level of society and were drawn from every conceivable situation and employment. It was a key moment in the development of Spanish modernity, as well as a ripe opportunity for an ambitious playwright to make his mark. Lope wasn't slow to recognise the commercial possibilities of the moment, and with his relentless productivity – frequently giving two new plays a week to the stage – he rapidly established himself as the undisputed giant of a Spanish theatre that was increasingly vibrant and commercially successful. 'So what if they criticise my plays and think that I wrote them for fame', he wrote. 'That was never the case. I wrote them for money.' He was certainly generous with the fortune that he earned, and the phrase 'es de Lope', meaning 'it's worthy of Lope', has passed into the language to denote the excellence of any gift or the quality of an item on sale. When he died, the whole of Madrid took to the streets for his funeral. So he got his fame too.

The population of this brash and driving new city had every reason to be grateful to Lope. By royal decree, the profits from the theatres were ploughed back into the public realm, particularly through major building projects, and Lope's work alone contributed greatly to the embellishment of the urban landscape. But, more than anything else, Lope had given his audiences a theatre of genuinely national proportions – comparable in scale, reach and scope to that of Elizabethan England. He created a space in which a people were able to think about themselves in front of themselves, allowing theatre to do what it does best, that is to encourage and enable the collaborative performance of collective meaning. Both as artist and impresario, Lope paid a great deal of attention to his own particular 'groundlings', giving them fast-moving pieces located within the heart of their own national story. Lope drew frequently on the country's history, its myths, the *topoi* of its collective imagination, and in doing so he invited his spectators to engage with and find meanings for their own experience in a city that, like them, was grappling with a process of self-definition.

It is no exaggeration to say that Lope made theatre happen in Spain. Of course, writers like Cervantes had been staging plays in the decades before Lope came to public notice (when he was in his late twenties), but without creating anything of real lasting worth. Lope kick-started the theatre by re-inventing it, just as Valle-Inclán was to do again, four centuries later. In a verse treatise, the accurately-entitled *New Art of Writing Plays,* Lope defended the concept of popular taste in the face of the classical theorists. He made there an early case for the freedom of the creative imagination, and, in doing so, was able to create a body of work that was limited only by what he had time to write. The by now largely stifled debate, like a tension in the air, between the rigid cosmic schemes and unmoving social codifications of the old order, and the more dynamic visions of the modern, sparked a profound response in Lope. In his play *Lo fingido verdadero* (*The Great Pretenders*) he is able to poke fun at Aristotle as a mere 'stickler for the rules', a rejection of classical fixity that allowed him to create a theatre whose liberated dramatic actions are still fresh four hundred years later. The freshness of Lope's theatre, then and now, derives in large part from the quality of the artistic space he created specifically for it.

THE DOG IN THE MANGER

All of that said, *The Dog in the Manger* – *El perro del hortelano,* written at some point between 1613 and 1615 – seems to observe the classical unities to a notable extent. But such observance is more apparent than real. It is true that over three-quarters of the action takes place within the palace of Diana, Countess of Belfor, situated in Naples, then part of the Spanish Empire. The time of the play seems also to be compressed into two or three days, as conventionally prescribed. In this case, however, the anguished lover Teodoro makes one or two brief references to time that has passed without the audience's awareness, almost *in absentia,* so that whatever period of time the action covers, the audience experiences it from the subjective point of view of the male protagonist – reminiscent of Shakespeare's so-called 'double time'. Simply, Lope refused to be bound by unities of time and place because, as an artist, his emphasis was on human relationships. In his theatre, these are always in the foreground, with the demands and constraints placed around them by their social context forming a very real background. And although his plays are acute observations of what today we would call the psychological dimension, that obscure layer that lies between what people say and what they hide, these relationships build up through story, through unstopping action that flows in a wholly dynamic manner from the interaction of characters and the performance of speeches that are in themselves actions, in that they cause things to happen and situations to change.

All of this makes for theatre at its most entertaining. In his essay 'The Slyness of Boredom', Peter Brook counsels us to be true to our boredom, to read our flagging attention as an accurate barometer of how well the play is being performed. Lope was aware of how easy – and with what disastrous consequences – it was to lose the volatile audiences of the Madrid theatres of his day, the 'corrales' which, not unlike the theatres of Elizabethan England, were like crammed and throbbing cockpits. And *The Dog in the Manger* is a particularly good example of the fast-moving stagecraft he developed in response. The play centres on a well-known literary *topos* – like Webster's *The Duchess of Malfi,* with which *The Dog in the Manger* shares several similarities, both of structure and of detail – which is that of love between social unequals. In the striving mélange that was Madrid society at the time, such a topic was bound to strike a chord. Indeed, the particular specifics of the debate that Lope is sparking in this play remain relevant almost four hundred years later. How is privilege achieved, and how is it maintained? What is the relationship between blood, blue blood and sex? What are the subterfuges that nobility will employ in order to maintain its privilege and its status? And the question that underlies it all: where does the principle of love, the bond of common humanity, sit with all of this?

The play is constructed along a series of transitional moments between fervent affirmations and frenzied denials. It sets up a series of brusque – at times bruising – encounters between social codes and driving desire. These are characters who are walking the emotional high-wire, without a safety net, characters who simultaneously perform – consciously and unconsciously – socially sanctioned modes of behaviour along with the impulse to shatter those modes. Lope was surely aware that that performance – by virtue both of its performative nature and of the special place in which it took place – would move from the stage, from that clearly defined cultural context, into the real life of his audience, clarifying in the process crucial issues about social hierarchy, the links between social and sexual power, economic dependency, and the dictates of duty. Theatre, for him, was a business. But it also had a purpose, and in that purpose he responded – again consciously and unconsciously – to a number of issues central to national life. The emotional roller-coaster that is *The Dog in the Manger,* in that sense, derives its energy both from the performance of typical assumptions about gender and social status, that actors would have played out, to huge emotional effect, to discrete areas of their segregated audience, and from the way that these assumptions are constantly offset by characters' desire, by the strategies they implement in order to venture beyond the bounds of the permissible. The beckoning of the dangerous world through the liminal space is dramatised here as the thrill of high-flying. And if that inevitably leads to a fall, the thrill of transgression remains with the spectator long after Icarus's wings have melted.

THE TRANSLATION

The Dog in the Manger is at once one of Lope's most controlled and most erotically liberated plays. The sense of eroticism evident in Diana and Teodoro's covert courtship, in turns teasing and brutal, pervades their entire relationship, with its suggestion of games of sexual power and domination. As we have already noted, Lope inevitably wrote his plays with a degree of self-censure. That knowledge has led to a fine new Spanish version of the play – what we might call an *intralingual* translation – by the writer Emilio Hernández, premiered recently in Madrid's Centro Cultural de la Villa. By describing his version as 'libertine but not free', Hernández is signalling his intention to render more explicit the implicit eroticism of the play, as well as affirming his belief that such 'writing forward' would be in keeping with Lope's practice if he were writing today. There is a point here. Performance always takes place in the here and now, and Hernández, like all theatre practitioners, is keen to avoid the sort of historicism that characterises some traditional academic approaches to theatre. But, in the case of *The Dog in the Manger*, Lope's self-censure is also that of his characters: this has led to a play that is constantly on the boil, and where characters are forever drawn into that dangerous area where words begin to mean real things, where real things are constantly on the verge of being said and of being understood. 'No matter what you say, say nothing' was Seamus Heaney's famous advice to a Northern Irish society divided against itself. And in this tense and dangerous House of Belflor (think of the sublimated eroticism in that name alone), where a whole host of passions are suddenly unleashed, no matter what they say, these characters are definitely saying something, when it would be much wiser to leave everything unsaid.

It is for those reasons that this version tries to resist the temptation to write forward in this manner. Within the constraints placed upon the translator by the fact that one is endeavouring to create a scaffold upon which the actors can build their performance, this version tries to remain as faithful as possible to the complex character interactions that lie at the heart of this play, re-constructing them as Lope constructed them. Where it has introduced some premeditated change, however, is with the formal qualities of the original. This is written in a variety of verse forms, each one of which communicates a different emotional tone to the audience, rather in the way that music is used today. A possibility is to try and re-create that ritualistic – almost ceremonial – polymetric element of the original, that outward and most visible sign of Lope's theatre. A number of academics have attempted such translations, with greater or lesser success, avowing their respect for forms that were perfectly adapted for audiences of nearly four hundred years ago. This translation, however, takes a different route. It certainly recognises the importance of heightened forms of expression in this hot-house world of heightened emotions, and most lines are given in eight beats, designed to impose order on speeches where thought and emotion characteristically flow together. Exceptions to this occur in shorter lines, usually five-beat, when characters are, for whatever reason, in emotional free-fall. The original play also offers a number of sonnets, either as *billets-doux* or at moments when characters speak from the very heart of their being – those moments of intense emotional revelation when, as Yeats put it, passion and precision become one in poetry. These sonnets are translated as sonnets in order to maintain something of that theatrical function.

None of this is meant to be taken as a statement of general principle about how translations should be written. But it is a statement about how this particular version emerged. There are two reasons why, as a translator, I think I have intervened less in the finished version of this play than I have felt was necessary or desirable in other translations I have written, including of a number of other plays by Lope de Vega. One is the emotional balance I have already referred to. The other has to do with the growing reception of Lope de Vega in this country. His plays – admittedly a tiny fraction of his extant plays, but some nonetheless – are published and performed in Britain much more than even just over a decade, when London's Gate Theatre launched its pioneering Spanish Golden Age season. Lope de Vega has now begun to negotiate a place for himself within the horizon of expectations of English-speaking theatre-goers. This doesn't mean that translators should stop producing creative translations and adaptations of his work. On the contrary, this is what keeps theatre vivid and alive. But we also have to let Lope speak for himself, and this translation is probably as faithful as the related demands of speakability and performance will allow.

David Johnston
Belfast, March 2004

ACKNOWLEDGMENTS

My thanks are due to a number of people. First, to Laurence Boswell, who directed this version of the play for the RSC. It's now over ten years since we worked together on the Gate's Spanish Golden Age Season, and the advent of email has given Laurence a terrifying weapon in his inexhaustible search for the best possible script. Dozens of detailed emails provided passionate and precise readings of Lope's play, and gave clear and valuable critiques of my own attempts to render it into English. Second, to the actors who performed this version with such commitment, and who made their own contributions in rehearsal to the development of this script. Third, to a number of friends – John Clifford, Jonathan Munby, Joe Farrell, Juan Mayorga, and my colleagues and friends at the Lyric Theatre in Belfast – whose own love and understanding of theatre has helped me to develop my own thoughts and responses, and with whom I've had many enjoyable discussions. Finally, to Jennifer, for not allowing me to get away with anything, even when I deserved to.

To Jennifer

Characters

DIANA, Countess of Belflor

TEODORO, Diana's Secretary

TRISTAN, Teodoro's lackey

OCTAVIO, Diana's Old Steward

FABIO, Her Servant

ANARDA, Her Lady-in-waiting

DOROTEA, Her Lady-in-waiting

MARCELA, Her Lady-in-waiting

The Marquis RICARDO

CELIO, Ricardo's Servant

Count FEDERICO, Diana's Cousin

LEONIDO, Federico's Servant

Count LUDOVICO

CAMILO, Ludovico's Advisor

ANTONELO, Lackey

FURIO, Lackey

LIRANO, Lackey

ACT ONE

TEODORO and TRISTAN, fleeing. TEODORO is wearing a brightly-coloured cloak.

TEODORO: Tristan, quick!

TRISTAN: That was a bollocks.

TEODORO: She recognize us?

TRISTAN: Yes, no, maybe.

As they leave, DIANA, Countess of Belflor, enters in pursuit.

DIANA: Wait, sir! Stand your ground! Wait I said!
This is an outrage! Come back, sir!
Stop where you are! Help me! Anyone!
Are you all asleep? Well, I'm not!
That was no ghost, no fantasy
conjured from some deceitful dream.
I saw him clear as day. Where are you?
Wake up, will you! I need help!

Enter a servant, FABIO.

FABIO: My lady called?

DIANA: Your lady called?
Your lady is blazing with rage
and you come coolly ambling along.
Dunderhead! Find out who it was
came out of that bedroom.

FABIO: That room?

DIANA: It's your feet I want to hear from.
Not you answering back.

FABIO: My feet?

DIANA: Move!
Find out who it was. I want his name.

FABIO runs off.

He'll pay for this outrage, this disgrace.

Enter OCTAVIO, DIANA's old steward.

OCTAVIO: I thought I heard my lady call
but then I thought: at so late an hour?

DIANA: In the middle of the storm, the calm!
The first to bed, the last to rise,
here you come, doddering along.
Men are marauding through my house,
strangers roaming in every room,
at the door of my own bedroom
– the nerve, the effrontery –
and my chivalrous protector,
my knight in shining armour, says:
'I thought I heard my lady call
but then I thought: at so late an hour?'
You're right, why would I be calling?
Go back to bed.

FABIO returns.

FABIO: He flew...like a hawk.
Into the dark.

DIANA: Anything strike you?

FABIO: Strike me?

DIANA: His cloak was very rich.

FABIO: His hat...his hat nearly struck me...

DIANA: I'm surrounded by simpletons!

FABIO: ...when he threw it, I mean at the lamp,
And he killed it. From the doorway,
he was standing in the doorway.
He pulled his sword... I heard it rasping.
So I stopped.

DIANA: He flew like a hawk...
while you stood and clucked like a chicken.

24

FABIO: What could I do?

DIANA: What could you do?
Of course...Stop him? Kill him, if need be?

OCTAVIO: What if it were some nobleman?
Your family name would be disgraced.
Best keep things behind locked doors.

DIANA: Nobleman?

OCTAVIO: Aren't there any number
of fine-born men here in Naples
who are desperate to marry you,
who are so foolhardy in love
they'd try any trick to see you?
You said he was wearing a cloak
and Fabio said he had a hat...

DIANA: So he must have been some noble,
bent on seeing me...And who bribed
my servants to allow him in,
being such a loyal and faithful bunch!
Mark my words: I'll find out who it was.
The hat...it had plumes...bring it here.

FABIO: It'll be gone.

DIANA: The hawk paused in mid-flight
to pick it up? Fool!

FABIO: I'll take a light.

He leaves.

DIANA: If one of my servants did this,
they'll be out of this house for good.

OCTAVIO: And they would have no cause for complaint.
My lady, if I may say so,
perhaps risking your righteous anger,
may I point out that rejection
inflames the heart, makes it bolder.
Your insistence on not marrying,
do you think it to be well-advised?

DIANA: What do you know?

OCTAVIO: What we all know:
that you're as set against marriage
as you are beautiful, my lady.
To be Count of Belflor's a prize
any man would give his eyes for.

FABIO returns.

FABIO: I found something.

DIANA: This thing's a hat?

FABIO: It's what he threw.

DIANA: This...thing?

OCTAVIO: Nasty.

DIANA: This is it...this is what you found?

FABIO: There was nothing else there, I swear.

OCTAVIO: So much for fine feathers.

FABIO: Burglar,
common thief.

OCTAVIO: Looks very like it.

FABIO: Running scared, miles away by now.

DIANA: This can't be right... I'm going mad.

FABIO: It's certainly the hat he threw.

DIANA: But it had feathers...great big plumes.
This piece of charred chicken carcass,
that you take for some burglar's cap,
it was a hat with fine feathers.

FABIO: It did, my lady, it did, but...
they were burnt off, went up like a torch,
when the hat flew into the lamp.
Wasn't it Icarus flew too close
to the sun and got his wings burnt,
so that he fell and drowned in the sea?
Well, the hat was like Icarus,

and the lamp was like the sun.
It flew too close, got its feathers burnt,
and down it went onto the stairs.
Not the sea.

DIANA: I'm in no mood for this.
I mean to find out who it was.

OCTAVIO: Always best to sleep on these things,
my lady. Time will tell.

DIANA: *What* time?
Nobody in this house shall rest
until we have the scoundrel's name.
Even if it's the last thing I do.
Get the women up.

FABIO leaves.

OCTAVIO: The women?
Surely, my lady, there's no need…

DIANA: There's every need! Some stranger,
had the free run of my house tonight.

OCTAVIO: Truth's sometimes better learned in secret.

DIANA: Sleep on a secret that time'll tell.
Very wise, Octavio. Thank you.

FABIO returns with some of the women of the household.

FABIO: I've brought you the important ones.
The rest are all dead to the world.
Only your ladies in waiting
were still awake.

ANARDA: We couldn't sleep.
(*Aside.*)   The storm. The sea's raging tonight.

OCTAVIO: Shall we withdraw?

DIANA: Yes. Go.

As they leave.

FABIO:	She's mad.
OCTAVIO:	She's on fire.
FABIO:	It's my arse got burnt.

They leave.

DIANA:	Dorotea.
DOROTEA:	Yes, my lady.
DIANA:	Which gentlemen frequent this street?
DOROTEA:	Mainly the Marquis and the Count.
DIANA:	Is that the truth? Don't lie to me,
	or it'll be the street you end up.
DOROTEA:	I would not lie.
DIANA:	What do they say?
DOROTEA:	I've never heard them speak, not once.
	May I burn in hell if that's not so.
DIANA:	You've seen them send notes? With servants?
DOROTEA:	No.
DIANA:	Go!
MARCELA:	Like the Inquisition.
ANARDA:	She's like the sea. She'll drown us all.
DIANA:	Anarda.
ANARDA:	My lady.
DIANA:	Who was it?
ANARDA:	Who?
DIANA:	Don't think I don't know your game.
	He bribed his way in, to see me.
	Who betrayed me?
ANARDA:	No one betrayed you.
	There's not one of us who would dare.
	You don't understand.
DIANA:	Understand?

Silence.

> It wasn't me he came to see.
> It was one of you!

ANARDA: My lady,
your indignation is proper
and though I am Marcela's friend,
I have to be honest with you.
There is a man in love with her,
and I believe she is with him,
though who he is, I don't know.

DIANA: You've told me that she stole the sheep.
No point in denying the lamb.

ANARDA: Why torture me for her secrets?
Some women may gossip, I don't.
He comes for Marcela, not you.
And it hasn't gone beyond talking.
You can calm down. There's no harm done.

DIANA: No harm done! My reputation?
An affair, going on, under my roof!
I am an unmarried woman!
If my father were still alive,
he'd have his head off his shoulders.

ANARDA: Let me explain, please…he's no stranger…
I mean the man that comes to see her
doesn't really *come* to see her.
So no one's honour's put at risk.

DIANA: He's a servant, then?

ANARDA: My lady.

DIANA: Who?

ANARDA: Teodoro.

DIANA: That's absurd.
Teodoro's my secretary.

ANARDA: They talk; that's all I know.

DIANA: They talk...
That's all, Anarda.

ANARDA: My lady,
be calm, I beg you.

DIANA: That will do!
He came to see another woman.
My honour is safe. I am calm.
Marcela!

MARCELA: My lady.

DIANA: So then...

As MARCELA and ANARDA cross.

MARCELA: She's going to skin me alive.

DIANA: ...it was you who compromised this house?

MARCELA: Whatever she told you, my lady,
my only loyalty is to you.

DIANA: Loyalty! You?

MARCELA: What have I done?
In what way have I offended?

DIANA: You talk to a man in my house,
in my chambers, and you wonder
how it is you've offended me!

MARCELA: Teodoro's such a lovely fool.
He comes out with all sorts of things,
the sorts of things that lovers say
he comes out with...by the dozen..

DIANA: By the dozen? Very fertile...
his imagination.

MARCELA: I mean,
it doesn't matter where we are,
what we're doing, his thoughts...translate
into such words.

DIANA: Strange word to use.
These translations, are they faithful?

30

MARCELA: My lady?

DIANA: His thoughts are just for you?
What does he say?

MARCELA: I don't recall.

DIANA: I think you do.

MARCELA: One day he'll say
'My soul swims through the dark river
of your eyes'. Then 'My soul drowns
in your absence, without you I die'.
And he begs for a strand of hair.
To bind his thoughts and words, he says.
What interest can such ravings have
for my lady?

DIANA: They interest *you*.

MARCELA: I believe his words are faithful
to what lies within. He loves me;
in a way that's honourable and true
since it has marriage as its goal.

DIANA: Then I approve of your desire.
Shall I arrange it?

MARCELA: My lady,
I could desire nothing more.
Your anger swiftly melts away,
in the warmth of your noble heart.
Let me tell you this: I love him.
He is the cleverest and best,
the wisest man in this city.

DIANA: I know. He's my secretary.

MARCELA: Although there can be no compare
between writing letters on business
and the warmer whisperings
of the heart.

DIANA: Yes. You shall marry,
when the time's ripe. You have my word.

But I cannot be less than I am.
My anger is both just and known,
and therefore I must sustain it.
There is no choice. Be more prudent
and I shall find the right moment.
Teodoro is a good man,
who's lived in this house all his life,
and I'm bound to you by kinship,
Marcela. I owe you both favour.

MARCELA: And I am your faithful servant.

DIANA: Go.

MARCELA: I kiss your feet.

DIANA: Leave me now.

ANARDA: Well?

MARCELA: I rode out the storm.

ANARDA: She knows?

MARCELA: Everything that there is to know.
And she's given us her blessing.

The three women curtsy and leave. DIANA is left alone.

DIANA: And there've been many times, at work, at rest,
I've bathed in his beauty's warmth, like the sun,
and felt how his grace and wit possessed
a charm that melts, or at least I would have done.
The property of our nature, they say's to love
but nature sits uneasy with honour and with name,
and though I might dream of swooping from above,
a noble birth regards low-born things with shame.
Envy, how well I know your sting,
living here as I watch the joy of others,
and though I feel this poor heart bursting,
I cling to rank, and memory smothers
everything but one resentful hope in store:
if only I were less, if only he were more.

She leaves. TEODORO and TRISTAN appear.

TEODORO: My heart's pounding!

TRISTAN: So it should be!
I'm terrified. I told you, wait,
until the Countess has gone to bed.
If she finds out that it was you,
you're a dead man. And did you listen?

TEODORO: Love is deaf.

TRISTAN: Dead men are deaf too.
You're all attack and no defence.

TEODORO: Rapier-sharp in love and war.
A master swordsman.

TEODORO executes an imaginary sword thrust.

TRISTAN: You think so?
A master swordsman calculates the odds,
works out the risk, thinks what he's doing.

TEODORO: She recognized me?

TRISTAN: Yes…and no.
She doesn't know, but she suspects.

TEODORO: When Fabio followed me downstairs…
it's a miracle he's still alive.

TRISTAN: And my hat trick?

TEODORO: That saved him.
He stopped. Or I'd have run him through.

TRISTAN: 'Lamp', says I, 'say we're strangers here.'
'You lie', says the lamp, bold as brass.
So I took my hat off to him
and settled the score there and then.
No lamp's going to call me a liar.
I think my honour's been avenged.

TEODORO: I *am* a dead man.

TRISTAN: You lovers,
            that's the sort of stuff you come out with,
            you bleat even before you're shorn.

TEODORO: So what else can I do, Tristan?
            This is a dangerous situation.

TRISTAN: I'll tell you what: you could forget
            Marcela for a start. Trust me.
            If the Countess knew it was you,
            you'd be out of here, on your ear.
            Or worse.

TEODORO: Forget her! Just like that?

TRISTAN: I could teach you a thing or two
            about taking love by the scruff.

TEODORO: More of your nonsense?

TRISTAN: It's an art-form.
            For your sanity's sake, yes and
            your career, pay attention.
            A guide to the art of not loving.
            First lesson: you have to forget,
            providing you also renounce hope.
            You must be firm in your intention,
            grit your teeth against your feelings.
            Hope clutters most things. Hope to love
            and you'll go and fall in love again.
            Where there is hope, there is no change.
            A question: why can't a man
            expel a woman from his mind,
            like he'd pluck a speck from his eye?
            Because, simply, it suits him
            to live in hope of going back.
            Such dreams keep the real world at bay.
            His imagination's a-whirl,
            like some crazed clock, striking odd hours,
            as his life spins out of control.
            Now imagine peace...quiet...hush
            the stillness of an unwound clock.

TEODORO: But memory stirs and winds the clock,
and feeling holds tight to its prize.

TRISTAN: Ah, as the poet rightly said:
'memory's the enemy within'.

TEODORO: Which poet?

TRISTAN: I don't read poetry.
The trick is: make memory serve you.

TEODORO: How?

TRISTAN: By thinking only of her flaws,
her defects, not her beauty and grace.
Therein lie wisdom and success.
It's the only way to cure yourself.
So, the next time you think of her,
elegantly dressed, tight-waisted,
on those high-heeled slipper things...
remember what some wise man said:
'Women's beauty is the product
of tailors and of alchemists.'
She owes more to the dressmaker
than to her real maker above.
And while she's dressed up to the nines,
or even tens, elevens and twelves,
yours is the eye of the penitent
steadfast and cured, purged of nonsense.
So remember what lies beneath –
like when you eat a cheap meat pie,
and you think of the butcher poking
round in the guts of some quartered thief –
and you'll soon lose your appetite.
For the woman, no less than the pie.
Disgust is the best medicine.

TEODORO: What would you know of medicine?
You're a quack, you've never studied.
Your cures might work for some peasant,
but I have a much finer eye.
and I see women as they are:
pure like the finest crystal glass.

TRISTAN: When they break, they cut like glass.
                  Experience has taught me well.
                  This handsome face in front of you
                  has known what it is to love;
                  a woman, well into her prime,
                  a large red imperfect creature
                  who numbered among many flaws
                  a belly the size of a planet.
                  She could grip clothes pegs in its folds;
                  she used to hide her money there;
                  you'll have heard of the village tree,
                  a big walnut, that was so big
                  that they made it into the jail,
                  well, her paunch was of similar scope.
                  so vast that she could rent it out
                  to travellers and homeless people.
                  And she used to overcharge them.
                  Did I mention what a liar
                  and a fraudster that woman was?
                  Was I not right to forget her?
                  But when I tried, lilies, jasmine,
                  marble and snow, flooded my mind,
                  and I dreamt of her in clinging skirts
                  and the sheerest of petticoats.
                  So I took my own medicine,
                  and thought instead of old bolsters,
                  stained and stuffed with old rough horse-hair,
                  of trunks crammed with greasy letters,
                  or of ripe pumpkins about to burst
                  and once I even... Perhaps not...
                  Anyway, love became disgust.
                  The paunch exploded, went pop in my mind.

TEODORO: Marcela is pure and lovely.
                  She will never go pop in my mind.

TRISTAN: Then her grace will be your disgrace.

TEODORO: What can I do, she's grace itself?

TRISTAN: Think too of the Countess's grace.
The sort that goes well with favour.
The sort you don't want to fall from.

DIANA appears.

DIANA: Teodoro...

TEODORO: It's her!

DIANA: A word.

TEODORO: My lady.

TRISTAN: What word? Out? All of us...four words.

DIANA: I have a friend, unskilled in writing,
who's asked me to compose this note,
a *billet-doux*; I felt I should,
I owe her that much as a friend,
but as I'm so unskilled in love,
I thought maybe you'd improve the style.
Take it, Teodoro, read it.

She hands him a paper.

TEODORO: What you've set your hand to, my lady,
will be beyond all improvement.
I do not dare presume.

DIANA: Read it.

TEODORO: Your modesty is excessive.
There is much I could learn from you.
I have had no dealings with love.

DIANA: Never...ever?

TEODORO: I am aware
of my own shortcomings too much.

DIANA: So aware that you cannot bear
to be seen? Such diffidence.
But you were seen last night – disguised.

TEODORO: Was I indeed? By whom, may I ask?

DIANA: Octavio saw you at midnight.

TEODORO: It must have been with Fabio then.
We're always playing little jokes.

DIANA: Read it.

TEODORO: Some enemy's said this,
someone who's envious of me.

DIANA: Jealous perhaps. Read the letter.

TEODORO: It'll be a work of art, I'm sure.

He reads.

To desire at the sight of desire,
to love because others love too,
is to burn in the flame of envy's fire;
impossible they say, but such love is true.
My heart stormed when he looked at her,
for love acknowledges no rank or birth,
but envies the knowledge her love's secure
because loving her is to deny my worth.
Heart churning with no rhyme, no reason,
love born from jealousy, deeply feeling
this is my love, and love's no treason.
I do not give way, nor resist; sealing
my lips but yet opening them wide to kiss.
Those with eyes to see, will see. They'll see this.

DIANA: Well?

TEODORO: If it serves the writer's purpose,
it's a model of its kind. But...
how can love be born of jealousy?
Love is the father, not the child.

DIANA: Then let us imagine the case:
this lady found the man pleasant,
but with no stirring of desire
until he looked at someone else,
and so from jealousy, love was born.
Is that possible?

TEODORO: Perhaps so.
But jealousy also has its source,

	and that source, I think, must be love.
	Cause and effect, essential logic.
DIANA:	Perhaps so. But I know my friend.
	Before, she'd enjoyed his company,
	but when she saw him love, and be loved,
	she cared less for her own good name
	than for the thousand desires
	that surrounded her like cruel thieves
	and left her stripped of her good name,
	alone and bare of good intentions.
TEODORO:	Your note is passionate. But precise.
	I do not dare try to match it.
DIANA:	I want you to try.
TEODORO:	I do not dare.
DIANA:	I'm asking you to...please.
TEODORO:	My lady,
	I'm afraid you'll find me wanting.
DIANA:	I'll wait here. Be quick.

TEODORO leaves.

Tristan!

TRISTAN:	Though I rush to be of service,
	my appearance, my lady,
	slows my step and makes me falter.
	My master, your secretary,
	is – how can I put it? – hard up,
	strapped for cash, broke, and he forgets
	that servants' clothes maketh the master,
	as some wise man once put it.
	I am that servant, his mirror,
	his harbinger and his herald,
	the ladder up which the eye travels,
	the onlooker's first port of call
	before gazing fully on him
	splendidly mounted on horseback.

DIANA: Does he gamble?

TRISTAN: I wish he did.
        If only he had such resource,
        for men who gamble are never short
        of a pretty penny, for this
        and for that. In times gone by,
        every king used to learn a trade
        so that they could earn a living
        even if the worst came to pass
        – you know, wars, exile, and the like.
        It's wise to learn to gamble young,
        because a gambler'll never starve.
        Work grinds people into the ground.
        No matter how much flair or skill
        you have, there's always someone who
        says simply your work's worth nothing;
        the artist honing, polishing,
        and perfecting over long years,
        some critic comes along and says 'No',
        and a lifetime's work is thrown away.
        But the gambler, he calls his bet
        and the money comes pouring in.
        All with very little effort.

DIANA: So not a gambler?

TRISTAN: Too cautious.

DIANA: A lover?

TRISTAN: Made of ice.

DIANA: Of ice?
        I find that hard to believe,
        with him being so young and handsome,
        surely there's been some harmless fling?

TRISTAN: I wouldn't know; I feed the horses.
          That's my job. And he works all day,
          and keeps his nose to the grindstone.

DIANA: And at night?

TRISTAN: He goes out alone.
I've got a broken hip.

DIANA: Oh dear.

TRISTAN: I don't want to make excuses
about walking into doors and things,
like I was some unfaithful wife,
explaining away the bruises,
but I fell... I fell down some stairs.
I counted each step with my ribs.

DIANA: That's what happens, you see, Tristan,
when you throw your hat at the lamp.

TRISTAN: Bloody hell! She knows the whole thing.

DIANA: Well?

TRISTAN: Ah...yes...I see what you mean.
It was a bat. Flying in here.
A great big gruesome thing, slimy
and shiny black, squeaking away.
This will disrupt my lady's rest,
I thought, so I threw my hat at it.
It hit the lamp – and in the dark
my feet went from under me and...
I shall spare you the injuries,
my lady, suffered in your service.

DIANA: And you went flying...in the dark.
The blood of such flying vermin
– of bats I mean – is greatly prized.
You can boil it into a broth,
mix it with some aromatic herbs,
and any liar who feeds on it
is compelled to confess the truth.
I shall have these bats' blood next time.
And perhaps serve the broth to you.
Go.

TRISTAN: My lady.

As he leaves.

DIANA: My mind's spinning.

TRISTAN: The bat's a rat and she smells it.
                And I'm caught like one in a trap.

Enter FABIO.

FABIO: My lady, Marquis Ricardo's here.

DIANA: Show him in.

Enter the Marquis RICARDO, with his servant CELIO.

RICARDO: Lovely Diana:
                There's no impediment love will not brook,
                no labour that for my love would be lost,
                no hindrance that would make my foot falter,
                speeding here to press my suit, declare my love.
                I know I have rivals more arrogant,
                who would think my ambition perhaps high,
                but the vessel of their love is empty
                whilst my cup overflows with love for you.
                Today you are so simply radiant,
                that my heart dances as my eyes look,
                and seeing you so lovely, so alive,
                I make no inquiry as to your health.
                This is the deep knowledge of the lover,
                entranced at the beauty of his beloved,
                and in that beauty he sees her health shine.
                Those who ask you if you're well do not see.
                They are fools, you should drum them from your
                    door.
                I see you are well and so in return
                I ask you to ask me how I am.

DIANA: Good sir,
                your wit leaves me almost without breath.
                To see me as being so alive
                and to deduce from that I'm well,
                is a notion both poetic and wise.
                As to your health, I daren't speculate.

RICARDO: A man's health, my dear, is in his honour,
and my intentions are honourable.
You may therefore speculate quite freely,
and indeed you'd have your family's blessing,
if such speculation became stronger.
Since your father's death you have been alone,
and they, like me, are waiting for but one word.
With my own pater's very recent demise
I've inherited great titles and estates,
but if I were to rule from north to south,
from the frozen wastes to the burning sands,
and from Aurora's rising in the east,
to where she takes her rest in the bloodshot west,
and had I all the gold that men worship,
treasure chests full of diamonds and pearls,
that rain of tears from the sea's depths,
– by which I mean pearls, lovely image, isn't it? –
then I would take them all and give them to you,
and I would fight single-handed with the sea
to serve you, Diana, you and you alone,
and I would walk the earth with feet of fire,
from here to antipodean shores,
to assert your beauty and sovereignty there.

DIANA: How could I fail to be impressed
by your gifts of…phraseology?
I shall turn your words in my mind,
though we must seek not to offend
the feelings of Count Federico.

RICARDO: Indeed, he wears his feelings on his sleeve,
a sleeve like the suit to which it is attached,
known to all for its sham plumes and false
      colours.
Feelings and suit superior to mine
in every way, except in quality.
And so I trust the justice of my suit
– I'm sure you noticed my little pun there –
will leave such shabbiness exposed.

TEODORO enters.

TEODORO: The letter.

RICARDO: You're busy. I shall go.

DIANA: If it were to the Pope himself,
you'd still be welcome.

RICARDO: Very tedious things,
long visits, when you've letters to see to.

DIANA: You've a ready wit.

RICARDO: Ready to serve you.

RICARDO and CELIO take their leave.

RICARDO: How did we do, Celio, do you think?

CELIO: I think your suit was pressed to a pulp,
my lord.

DIANA: You've written it?

TEODORO: I have,
as you ordered. With no confidence.

*DIANA stretches out her hand and TEODORO gives the letter
to her. She reads.*

DIANA: We see others love, and we wish to love too.
But the feelings born from envy's gaze corrode,
for love engenders love, and love proves true
only when the heart and mind are pre-disposed.
In love's genealogy, envy has no place
for what envy conceives is born defiled
But where jealousy brings fire to the face
there is love, for jealousy is love's natural child.
I shall say no more for fear that offence
is given all too easily to one above,
even though such fears offer no defence
when I turn my face away from the child of love.
If I intimate that I am somehow deserving
how may I appear, other than just self-serving?

Carefully composed.

TEODORO:　　　　　　　You're making fun.

DIANA:　　　I wish I could.

TEODORO:　　　　　　What do you mean?

DIANA:　　　Yours is better.

TEODORO:　　　　　　　Then I'm sorry.
There's a point of principle here.
A servant will fall from favour
if he proves wiser than his master.
There's the story of a certain king
and his favourite secretary.
He called him aside and told him,
'I've had difficulty with a letter,
and although I have written it,
I want you to write another,
so that I can choose which one is best'.
The man did his master's bidding,
and when the king said 'Yours is better',
he rushed home and said to his son,
the eldest of the three he had,
'My life's in danger, we must flee.
We must leave the country at once.'
'Father, why?' asked the boy in fear.
'The king knows I'm cleverer than he.'

DIANA:　　　There's no comparison at all.
For although yours is well composed,
it follows the concept I laid down.
Because I find your pen pleasing,
do not assume I think mine dull.
As a woman, I make mistakes
and at times may lack wisdom,
but your fear offence is given
all too easily to one above,
I find contrary to reason.
How can an inferior offend,
loving well? Loving ill's the offence.

TEODORO: The reason of the natural order,
            but when men strive, order changes.
            Think of the paintings of Phaeton
            and Icarus falling from the skies,
            Phaeton drawn by golden horses
            to a high cliff top, then hurled down,
            and Icarus, his wings of wax
            scorched in the crucible of the sun.

DIANA: Killed by Zeus…killed by the sun.
            You serve a woman, so be bold.
            Love is simply perseverance,
            and women are not made of stone.
            I shall take this. And read it
            at my leisure.

TEODORO: It's deeply flawed.

DIANA: Not that I see.

TEODORO: Take yours.

DIANA: Keep it.

            No, destroy it.

TEODORO: Destroy it, why?

DIANA: Its loss would be no great matter.
            There's much more than that may be lost.

She leaves.

TEODORO: Who'd have thought it? Perhaps I'm wrong.
            It seems so out of character,
            this sudden…impetuosity.
            'There's much more than that may be lost.'
            What may be lost? Her friend? Herself…
            The friend's a masquerade…it's her.
            How can it be? Nothing touches her,
            so proud, so high, and this letter
            professes everything she's not.
            She's not some fool to go rushing in
            or lovestruck girl to lose her command.

The finest men in Naples court her,
princes, noblemen...whose laces
they'd say I wasn't fit to tie.
I'm in danger here. This is a plot.
She knows that I love Marcela –
she's testing me...tempting me...
But if she's leading me on, why?
She blushed, her face lit like a flame
and her voice trembled when she said
'There's much more than that may be lost'.
She blushed like a rose in the dawn,
opening its petals like red lips,
brushed with the moisture of the dew.
Her face coloured like an apple
that's ripening in the summer sun...
What I've seen here, and what I've heard,
I think...God knows, I may be mad...
is too much to be some joke or test.
But too little too to be passion.
But my thoughts are flying away,
dreaming already of great things:
one thing's true: she's so lovely.
She's beautiful and she's clever.
Diana, Diana...beyond compare.

MARCELA appears.

MARCELA: Teodoro, can we talk?

TEODORO: My love,
what could ever stop us talking?
I'd move mountains for you, die for you.

MARCELA: I died a thousand times last night
waiting for dawn, like a tiny bird
lost in the dark, too scared to move,
but when dawn came flaring in the sky,
like Apollo stirred by Aurora,
my heart sang and I thought to myself:
'Soon I shall see my Apollo'.

I have things to tell you. She knows.
She wouldn't rest till she found out,
from so-called friends whose envy
of my joy and my happiness
helped loosen tongues already loose.
There's no honour among servants,
and there's no friendship that's sincere.
Diana's restless like the moon,
never sleeping, always watching,
she came out and saw our secret.
No...no...no...don't panic, my love,
for it will all be for the best.
I told her you want to marry me,
that you desire no one else,
and I told her how tenderly
I adore you, and I praised you
to the heavens – your grace, your wit,
your virtues, your style, your beauty...
She is indeed a great lady
– she is more, she is a goddess –
because she rejoiced for us both,
and earnestly gave me her word
– she swore we'd be married. She swore!
At the very earliest chance,
she said, she'd arrange our wedding.
I thought she would have flared with rage,
brought the whole house down around us,
and had us drummed onto the street...
but no...she's so serene of blood,
so noble, so wise, so perfect
that she acknowledges your worth.
Any servant with such a mistress
should count himself blest, Amen.

TEODORO: She said she'd arrange our wedding?

MARCELA: She owes us favour.

TEODORO: Yes, she does,
and I was a fool to think other,

to even dream she spoke of me.
No high-flying hawk'd swoop so low
for prey like me.

MARCELA: You're muttering.

TEODORO: Simply babbling with joy, my love.
We spoke. She gave no indication
she knows it was me left your room
last night, cloaked and muffled...she knows?

MARCELA: She's being discreet, for if she knew –
that is, if she knew officially –
she'd have no choice but to punish us.
Although some might say that marriage
is the most divine of punishments.

TEODORO: And the most divine of cures.

MARCELA: Do you want to?

TEODORO: I'm a lucky man.

MARCELA: Acknowledge receipt.

TEODORO: With these arms,
the flourishes and curlicues
of love's pen and love's composition,
sealed with the signature of a kiss.

MARCELA: My secretary...

DIANA enters.

DIANA: My servants...
it always warms one's heart to see
how one's concern improves others
and leads them to amend their ways.
Don't stop, please. Not on my account.

TEODORO: My lady... Marcela and I...
I mean I was embracing her
out of pure joy, very pure joy,
when she told me of your favour
and kindness in blessing our love.
I left here last night in distress,

thinking that you, my lady, would think
that my honourable intentions
were dishonourable to you.
So I cannot, and will not lie
and say there was dust in her eye,
or that I was comforting her.
You, my lady, deserve the truth.

DIANA: And what is the truth, Teodoro?
Your abuse of my house last night?
Your disloyalty? My kindness,
as you term it, is it just cause
for this display of shamelessness?
When love descends to this low point,
there's no possible grace or favour.
Until your wedding, Marcela,
you'll be kept under lock and key.
Your example is unseemly.
Dorotea! I have no wish
to witness my other servants
begin cavorting like you.
Dorotea!

DOROTEA enters.

DOROTEA: My lady?

DIANA: Go with her to her room.
Take this key and then lock her in.
She can busy herself sewing.
But let one thing be very clear:
I'm not doing this out of anger.

As DOROTEA and MARCELA leave.

DOROTEA: What's going on?

MARCELA: She's a tyrant.
and our star's fallen very low.
She's got our whole life in her hands,
and she's going to lock me away
because of Teodoro.

DOROTEA: Jealousy can't keep you locked in.
Love's the best master key there is.
Except for this one, which I have.
So don't worry about being locked up.

They leave.

DIANA: You want to marry Marcela?

TEODORO: I would do nothing, my lady,
that causes you displeasure,
and I trust that you understand
that my offence was not so great
as some here'd have you think. You know
envy's painted with a scorpion's tongue,
and if Ovid had been a servant,
he'd have placed envy's dark abode
not in the country or the mountains,
but right here, in this scorpion's nest.

DIANA: So you don't love Marcela then?

TEODORO: I could live without her.

DIANA: Really?
She says you've lost your wits for her.

TEODORO: It's no real loss. They're not great wits.
But I would have my lady know
that Marcela's undoubted charms
have awoken no response in me.

DIANA: So you've made no pretty speeches,
whispered no blandishments that might
beguile a lady who's better born.

TEODORO: Words, my lady, come cheap.

DIANA: Tell me,
secretary, this way with words,
how does it work? What do you say?

TEODORO: You wrap a single truth – if that –
in the clothing of a thousand lies;
and you wrap that, in turn, in sighs.

DIANA: What words, exactly?

TEODORO: You push me,
my lady. 'Your eyes,' I told her,
'are the moons that light my night,
guiding me to the coral of your
celestial mouth.'

DIANA: Celestial? Her mouth?

TEODORO: Indeed, my lady, such language
features in the standard repertoire
of all lovers.

DIANA: You disappoint me.
I expected…more discernment.
I clearly have the finer eye,
because I see Marcela's flaws
outnumber her good points by far.
I mean her lips, coral? Blowzy,
ruddy, florid, lobster-red, yes.
More than once, you know I've had cause
to bring matters of, well, hygiene,
to her attention, women's things.
I'm sure you know…perhaps you don't.
Love is blind, and you love her so much.
The things I could tell you about her,
but perhaps we should say no more
about her charms. Or lack of them.
I want you to love and marry her,
and I'm sure you'll both be…in bliss.
As you're such a learned lover,
I want your advice…this lady,
my friend, of whom I spoke before,
greatly fears that she is in love.
Fears, because he's of low estate,
a commoner whom it would be
dishonourable for her to love.
The very thought is repugnant,
and yet, if she were to lose him,
she'd be consumed by jealousy.

He has no idea of her passion,
and treats her with due deference,
so much deference that...it's choking.

TEODORO: My lady, I'm not qualified
to speak on matters such as this.
I'm out of my depth, I swear.

DIANA: But you love Marcela, don't you?
All the lilies your tongue's been gilding.
If walls could speak...

TEODORO: They'd say nothing.

DIANA: You blush. Colour speaks louder than words.

TEODORO: Because we're making mountains here.
She gave her hand... I gave it back.
She has no grounds for complaint.

DIANA: She gave her hand...and you kissed it...
Like the chalice of wine at mass –
her hand passes from mouth to mouth.

TEODORO: Marcela's a fool; I confess
that I did dare to cool my own lips
– although not without some unease –
on the lilies and snow of her hand.

DIANA: Lilies and snow. I'm glad to know
how well they seem to cool passion.
What advice have you got for me?

TEODORO: The lady...of whom we both speak...
desires a man beneath her...
sorry, my lady, poorly put,
I am, as you see, unskilled...
She fears that to indulge her passion
would bring dishonour to her name.
Then she should love him with no name...
sleep with him anonymously.
Some sort of trick. A mask maybe.

DIANA: If he recognises her...have him killed?

TEODORO: The case of Marcus Aurelius
is pertinent in this respect…
He cooled his wife Faustina's desire
for a well-known gladiator
by having him slaughtered in the ring
and giving her his blood to drink.
Hardly a Christian example.

DIANA: As you say, we live in different times.
Where are the Lucretias of our days?
Or a Torquatus or Virginius?
Living examples of goodness,
of chastity and of honour.
But of course they had their Faustinas
to deal with, their wayward women,
their Poppeas and Messalinas,
who were so quick to forget themselves…
Write me a memoir on the subject.

She turns to go, stumbles and falls.

What are you doing standing there,
each arm the length of the other?
I've fallen. Here give me your hand.

TEODORO: I didn't dare to offer it.
Out of respect.

He wraps his hand in his cloak, and stretches out his hand.

DIANA: How very quaint.

TEODORO: It's how Octavio offers his,
when you're going to mass.

DIANA: His hand's old,
seventy years old, with liver spots.
It's a hand more dead than alive.
He cloaks his hand when he touches me
out of hygiene, not courtesy.
If you heard a friend cry for help,
imagine that they were drowning,
would you waste time looking for your cloak?

> Whatever protocol prescribes,
> an honest hand's an open one.
> It has no need to hide its face.

She offers her bare hand to TEODORO who, in turn, bares his.

TEODORO: Yours is a noble touch.

DIANA: One day,
> when you've spent a lifetime in this house,
> you'll offer your hand in your cloak.
> But, for now, you're my secretary.
> And you'll keep my fall a secret
> if you've any ambition to rise.

She leaves.

TEODORO: So maybe, and then maybe not, who knows?
> A woman though, and the certainty's remained
> that her face flushed the colour of a rose
> when she touched my hand, then the colour
>   drained.
> And she trembled, I felt her shake, but yet,
> I am unsure, for this is unknown ground.
> But this is the pathway to a prize so great
> that I must step forward to seize the crown.
> Marcela…to desert her would be unjust,
> to break her heart, leave her trust in tatters.
> I must stop. And think about these matters.
> On balance: women leave men in the flash of
>   an eye.
> If women live by the sword, that's how women
>   should die.

ACT TWO

Count FEDERICO and his servant, LEONIDO, outside a church.

FEDERICO: You saw her go in?

LEONIDO: As the dawn
enters the new day, its light spreading
across the fields, embroidering
them with flowers like a tapestry.
I doubt she'll be in there long though.
Galloping Don Pedro's singing mass.

FEDERICO: If only I could speak to her.

LEONIDO: You're her cousin. She can't refuse.

FEDERICO: Since I asked her to marry me,
she backs off, she shies away.
When I was simply her cousin,
we would spend whole days together,
with not a thought for…such things.
But when a man declares his love,
though she avoids everyone else,
she shuns him more, he sees her less,
and he has to engineer meetings
like this, waiting on street corners.
That's what's happened to me with her.
Loving her means that I've lost her,
and all passion brings is despair.
I was much happier before
when I was only her cousin.

The Marquis RICARDO and CELIO appear.

CELIO: She came on foot. With her household.

RICARDO: Her sweet footfall honours the street.

CELIO: Like the sun rising in the morning,
and picking out in its golden beams
the twin horns of heavenly Taurus,

	so the day is adorned with two stars,
	the two eyes of Countess Diana.
RICARDO:	My love has lent you eloquence.
	You do well to see her as the sun,
	for each suitor of Diana,
	the heavenly Diana,
	is a simple constellation,
	that together form her zodiac.
CELIO:	So who will be her Taurus?
RICARDO:	We'll let him be her Taurus.
	For it'll be him she speaks to first,
	just as the sun lights Taurus first,
	before entering the house of Leo.
	I think I'm a perfect Lion,
	And he who's lit last is lit longest.
	And we'll geld the bull…in the dark.
FEDERICO:	Not Ricardo!
LEONIDO:	Yes it is.
FEDERICO:	*Quelle surprise.*
LEONIDO:	He certainly looks the part today.
FEDERICO:	What do you mean?
LEONIDO:	He's well turned out.
FEDERICO:	You sound more jealous than me.
LEONIDO:	You?
	You're jealous?
FEDERICO:	Yes!
LEONIDO:	I didn't know.
	Jealous of what? She loves no one.
FEDERICO:	Jealous she might go and choose him:
	she is a woman after all.
LEONIDO:	But so vain she detests you all,
	equally.
FEDERICO:	Beauty is arrogant!

LEONIDO: But disdain is its ugly face...

CELIO: I think that's them coming out now.

RICARDO: The sun!

CELIO: Now's your chance.

FEDERICO: The dawn!

LEONIDO: Say something.

Enter DIANA, accompanied by all her servants, except TRISTAN. She sweeps by.

FEDERICO: I've been waiting here,
hoping we might happen to meet.

DIANA: Count Federico, how very kind.

RICARDO: And I've been waiting no less time,
hoping too that we might...chance one
upon the other.

DIANA: Happy chance,
Marquis Ricardo.

RICARDO: Happy indeed.

FEDERICO: There...she's as good as chosen him!

LEONIDO: Make her change her mind. Say something!

FEDERICO: Why would a man speak, Leonido,
when he knows no one's listening?

DIANA and her servants sweep past without pausing. TEODORO remains.

TEODORO: My beautiful thoughts,
rising and pitching,
you rise like a bird,
and I love your flight.
Yours is the madness
of gulls and starlings,
spinning and churning.
Though I call you home
I still urge you on,

upwards to the sun.
And I may well claim
your flight's unfounded,
that the race is lost,
but you rise higher,
the untethered dreams
of an infinite prize
beckoning you on.
You love your mistress.
Reason's a blindfold,
and you have eyes that see.
Tell your eyes, my thoughts,
they're building towers of gold
on top of beds of sand.
If we crash to earth,
it's your eyes I'll blame.
Though your eyes are mine
and I see your dream;
you dream what I hope.
And you could blame me.
My heart made you soar,
sent you to such heights,
far above the scope
of a low-born man.
So I have no right
to sit in judgment;
I am your madness,
as guilty as you,
as wild in my dreams,
and I fly with you.
It's time for resolve,
and should we be lost,
we're lost together.
You died for my dreams
while I gladly followed,
both of us flying blind.
Fly with my blessing,
for if you lose well

it will be no loss.
To count victory sure,
to act only when
the winning's certain
is the sane man's mark.
This is a great cause
and if I lose myself
I'll be well lost.
Others will envy
the glory of this venture.

TRISTAN arrives.

TRISTAN: I hate to intrude. A letter,
from Marcela, pining for you
in her solitary confinement.
It is heavy with her sighing;
even so, I don't expect payment.
At court everyone steers well clear
of people they no longer need.
It's only when a man's in favour,
as you clearly think you are,
he's beset by unwelcome callers.
But fortune's a fickle thing,
and when he falls from favour,
others just turn their back on them,
and walk away, like he had the plague.
Perhaps Marcela has the plague?
Maybe we should disinfect this?

TEODORO: Between you and the letter, I've both:
plague and an unwelcome caller.
Your breath's enough to disinfect it.

He reads.

'My dearest husband…' What? Husband!
How dare she? Sheer stupidity!

TRISTAN: The sheerest.

TEODORO: I've come much too far
                 to be concerned by some moth
                 still hovering round a candle.

TRISTAN: I think you should read the letter,
                 and not act so high and mighty.
                 Wine attracts flies, and wine's not scorned.
                 I remember when your hovering moth
                 was a soaring eagle in your eyes.

TEODORO: It's me who's aiming high, not her.
                 She's almost disappeared from view.

TRISTAN: My heart bleeds. So no reply then?

TEODORO: Only this.

He rips the letter in two and lets the pieces fall to the ground.

TRISTAN: That was brutal.

TEODORO: It was quick.

TRISTAN: It was unkind.

TEODORO: Things have changed. I've changed…utterly.

TRISTAN: Lovers are like apothecaries.
                 You have your illnesses and cures,
                 and you dress both up in hocus-pocus,
                 in your prescriptions and lovers' notes.
                 An attack of lover's colic: grease
                 of unctuous floralis, liberally applied
                 to the affected parts; *viz*, the heart.
                 Disdain: sirupus maximus,
                 to shift the blockage, ease the passage.
                 Lovers have to be regular,
                 or disdain – *viz*, nausea amorosa –
                 will harden the softest arteries.
                 Absence: poultice of frigidalis
                 that makes the heart not grow fonder.
                 Marriage: luna honeya for a week,
                 and after that you purge it
                 with dyspepsia infidelis.

And whether the patient lives or dies,
the reckoning comes, the account is closed
and the prescriptions just torn up.
And that's it; and that's what you've done.
You've closed your account with Marcela
and you've torn up her prescription,
without knowing what was in it,
whether it was kill or cure.
I believe I've made myself clear.

TEODORO: You've been drinking.

TRISTAN: You've been dreaming.

TEODORO: Seeing you're so good at Latin,
Tristan, try this: *carpe diem.*
No? Well it means to seize the day.
I will be the Count of Belflor,
or I shall die in the attempt.

TRISTAN: Caesar Borgia had a motto
emblazoned on his coat of arms:
'I shall be Caesar or nothing'.
But when everything fell apart,
when all his plans came to nothing,
some smart-arse came along and quipped:
'I'll be Caesar or nothing you said,
and you've succeeded in being both'.

TEODORO: I shall take up where he left off.
Failure and success together
on Fortune's wheel.

MARCELA and DOROTEA enter.

It's Marcela!

DOROTEA: If anyone has sympathy,
of all the Countess's servants,
it's me.

MARCELA: And I'm grateful to you.
If it weren't for your friendship
when I was locked up, I'd have gone mad.

I'll not forget. As for Anarda,
she doesn't know I know she's in love.
With Fabio. She's the cause of this,
telling the Countess about us.

DOROTEA: There's Teodoro!

MARCELA: My darling!

TEODORO: Marcela, please.

MARCELA: I adore you
and here you are.

TEODORO: Decorum, please.

MARCELA: I've been counting the days to see you.

TEODORO: That may be so, but walls have ears
and tapestries have eyes to see.
That's why there are figures on them.
To remind us we're being watched.
History gives us a clear warning.
A mute boy, the son of Croesus,
when he saw his father murdered,
was able to speak and call out
the names of his father's killers.
So the mute figures on these walls
may break their silence any time.

MARCELA: You read my note.

TEODORO: I tore it up.
And with it, I tore up our love.
I've learned a very hard lesson.

MARCELA: Are these the pieces?

TEODORO: Yes.

MARCELA: Of our love?

TEODORO: What alternative do we have?
Always looking over our shoulders.

MARCELA: What do you mean?

TEODORO: What I'm saying.
          I'll not upset the Countess again.

MARCELA: Decorum matters more than love?
          I should have known.

TEODORO: We can be friends;
          more than friends, we can be colleagues.

DOROTEA: How can you say that to Marcela?

TEODORO: How can I say it? Because it's true!
          This house has made me what I am,
          and I owe it all due respect.

MARCELA: Listen...

TEODORO: Let me be.

MARCELA: I love you.
          Why are you treating me like this?

TEODORO: This behaviour's inappropriate.

TEODORO leaves.

MARCELA: Tristan, Tristan!

TRISTAN: What?

MARCELA: What's wrong with him?

TRISTAN: He's behaving like a woman.

MARCELA: What woman'd behave like this?

TRISTAN: One who's made of honey...and gall.

MARCELA: Tell him...

TRISTAN: Me? I tell him nothing.
          I am the scabbard to his sword,
          seal to his letter, box to his hat
          I am the cloak that keeps him dry,
          I am his shadow, his two-step,
          the July he dreams of in February,
          the courier's horse, the summer storm...
          the tail that soars behind his comet.
          I am the nail on his finger

and if anyone cuts me off,
then that's all I'll be: a broken nail.
A nail discarded on the ground.

TRISTAN hurries out.

MARCELA: My God.

DOROTEA: What can I say?

MARCELA: The truth.

DOROTEA: I daren't.

MARCELA: I do.

DOROTEA: You shouldn't.

MARCELA: I should.

DOROTEA: What he said, about these tapestries...

MARCELA: Love when it's angry knows no bounds.
It pays no heed to any danger.
You'd think he'd designs on the Countess,
if it wasn't for her arrogance.
And yet, there must be some reason
why he's enjoyed her favour of late

DOROTEA: Be careful what you say: you're angry.

MARCELA: Angry? But not such a fool
that I won't take my revenge.

She sees FABIO, who has just arrived.

What?

FABIO: The secretary...is he here?

MARCELA: Is that some sort of joke?

FABIO: A joke?
My lady sent me to fetch him.

MARCELA: Then you must ask Dorotea.
I never speak to him, or of him.
He's the most tedious man I know.

FABIO: What are you two up to? I know you,
and I know when you're up to something.

MARCELA: Oh, we're up to something all right.

FABIO: You're trying to make fun of me...
You've always had an eye for him.

MARCELA: I listened to his nonsense, that's all.
But I'm in love with a real man.
A man like you.

FABIO: A man like me?

MARCELA: Are you not like you?

FABIO: Like me? Yes...

MARCELA: If I say a false word to you,
if I'm not mad for you, obsessed
by you, if I'm not yours, dear Fabio,
then I will be punished gladly
in the cruellest possible way.
I shall die of unrequited love.

FABIO: Is this some sudden conversion,
a death-bed scene where you make amends
for all your past disdain and scorn?
You broke my heart once before.
Maybe you are dying...or playing
with me again.

DOROTEA: This is your chance.
Do you not see she needs to love you?

FABIO: Needs to? What about wanting to?

DOROTEA: Teodoro's flying high. He's dropped her.

FABIO: I'm going to look for him, Marcela.
I'm good enough when he says no.
Love's turned you into a letter,
with his name on the envelope;
and if Teodoro's not at home,
just forward me to Fabio.

>   Then here's my reply: I accept
>   your letter. Yours as ever,
>   for better or for worse, Fabio.

He leaves.

DOROTEA: What have you done?

MARCELA: It just came out.
            But I don't care. What's there to lose?
            Anarda is in love with Fabio,
            isn't she?

DOROTEA: Yes, she is.

MARCELA: Well then,
            I'll have my revenge on them both.
            Isn't love the god of revenge?

DIANA and ANARDA enter.

DIANA: I will not be scolded like this.

ANARDA: With all due respect, my lady,
            what you've said, I don't understand.
            Marcela's here, with Dorotea.

DIANA: She's the last person I want to see.
            Marcela, go to your room.

MARCELA: Yes, my lady. Dorotea,
            will you come with me?

As they leave.

>   I told you.
>   She hates me...or else she's frightened.

ANARDA: May I speak?

DIANA: You may.

ANARDA: My lady,
            I say this out of love for you.
            Your two suitors you've just sent home...
            You're colder than Artemis,
            more intolerant than Lucretia.

She who disdains ends up disdained.
The Marquis and Count adore you.
Yet you treat them like untouchables.

DIANA: I'm tired of listening to you.

ANARDA: But who are you going to marry?
The Marquis is rich beyond desire,
and a very powerful man.
And Federico, your cousin,
any woman would die for him.
Yet you dismiss them out of hand.

DIANA: One's insane, the other a fool,
and you a greater fool than both.
Don't you realise? I am in love.
But with someone impossible.

ANARDA: You, in love? Who would have thought it!

DIANA: Am I not a woman?

ANARDA: Yes, but...

DIANA: But?

ANARDA: But a woman carved from ice,
that not even the sun could melt.

DIANA: Well. I've melted, and at the feet
of a man I cannot love.

ANARDA: How so?

DIANA: He is a man...of humble birth.

ANARDA: Who? If I may make so bold to...

DIANA: I am ashamed. I cannot say.

ANARDA: Why?

DIANA: He would destroy my honour.

ANARDA: Women love monsters of all kinds:
Pasiphae was in love with a bull;
Semiramis her horse; and others
so beyond belief I dare not say...
What harm's there in loving a man?

68

DIANA:	I fell in love. I can fall out. And that will be an end to it.
ANARDA:	An end? As easily as that?
DIANA:	If I turn my mind to it, yes. I have no wish to be in love. So I won't.

Music off.

What's that music?

ANARDA:	It's Fabio and Clara. Listen.
DIANA:	Let's hope they can brighten my mood.
ANARDA:	He's a lovely voice…don't you think?

Song off.

SINGER:	Oh who could ever do it Oh whoever did Not wanting to love Could hate instead
ANARDA:	The song contradicts your resolve.
DIANA:	But it's only a song. I know myself and I know my condition.
DIANA:	Love and hate are both in my hand.
ANARDA:	Is any woman so powerful, my lady?

TEODORO enters and ANARDA leaves.

TEODORO:	You want me, my lady?
DIANA:	A long time ago, I wanted you.
TEODORO:	I am here to do as you wish. Forgive me if I have been slow.
DIANA:	I take it you saw my admirers.
TEODORO:	I did.
DIANA:	Handsome, noble men, yes?

TEODORO: Very.

DIANA: Well, then, here's the question.
Which one should I choose?

TEODORO: My lady?

DIANA: I would value your opinion.

TEODORO: These are matters of personal taste.
And I would accept either man
as the better master.

DIANA: Poor advice
on such an important matter.
Is this how you repay my trust?

TEODORO: My lady, there are other men
in your household more qualified.
Octavio's better placed to advise.
He has a lifetime's experience
and, of course, the wisdom of age.

DIANA: Don't misunderstand me, Teodoro.
The man who will be your master,
I simply want you to like him.
So the Marquis or my cousin?
I think the Marquis is...handsome,
fine-figured. Do you not agree?

TEODORO: I agree.

DIANA: The Marquis it is then.
You can take him the happy news,
My Belflor's his, for the taking.
Go and tell him. He'll reward you well.

She leaves.

TEODORO: What disaster's this?
What dream died so quick?
A man's no angel
to soar to the sun;
my wings are scorched.
Diana's awake,

her feet on the ground,
while I'm in free-fall,
a fool for trusting
her promise of love.
Love can't conquer birth.
Her eyes bewitched me,
eyes that would have drawn
Ulysses from his course.
But I chose to dream
and the fault is mine.
I've lost her; she's gone,
But what's lost exactly?
What I never had.
I've lost an illness,
which while it lasted,
I imagined things.
I've lost the fever.
Time for some balance;
no more Count Belflor,
I've come back to earth
to a familiar shore.
Marcela'll be mine,
and let the Countess
marry her lord.
For love's only love
among two equals.
My dreams were born of air,
to air they return.
I shall dream no more,
for I lack merit
and without merit
you dream and you fall.

FABIO comes in.

FABIO: You've spoken to her?

TEODORO: Yes, I have,
              and I'm delighted at the news.
              The Countess has announced her marriage.

Both of the suitors you've just seen,
are fine gentlemen, who adore her,
but she, with typical discernment,
has chosen the Marquis.

FABIO: Good choice.

TEODORO: And, moreover, she has charged me
to take the news direct to him.
Believe me, he'll reward me well.
But I'd like you to go instead;
You and I have always been friends.
My joy's reward enough for me.

FABIO: I'm surprised, but no less grateful,
both for telling me such good news
and for this generous gesture.
I'll go to his house straightaway.
He'll be beside himself with joy.

FABIO leaves as TRISTAN enters.

TRISTAN: Is it true?

TEODORO: If it's bad, it must be.

TRISTAN: I saw them both, on my way in,
They're a pair of cracked bells, chiming
relentlessly in her ear,
filling her head with their dinging
and donging. No wonder she's fed up.
So it's true? She's chosen one?

TEODORO: Yes, Tristan, she was here just now.
That spinning sunflower, that weathervane
jiggling in every passing breeze,
that clouded mirror, that river
that doubles back on its own course,
that Diana, that moon waxing
and waning, that evil-eyed temptress,
that monster of capriciousness,
that woman who sought to destroy me,
to add me to her list of conquests,

d'you know what she did? She asked me
which of them I thought was better,
she'd not marry without my advice!
Can you imagine, I was speechless.
She told me she liked the Marquis
and sent me to break the good news.

TRISTAN: So she is married?

TEODORO: Ricardo.

TRISTAN: The Marquis...far be it from me
to say, Teodoro, I told you so;
wounds are sore enough without salt,
but you have been a real pillock.
Look at me... I'm going to be the Count.

TEODORO: Out for the count, more like. I'm done.

TRISTAN: You've only got yourself to blame.

TEODORO: I know. I looked into her eyes
and trusted her.

TRISTAN: A woman's eyes!
No greater poison to mortal sense!

TEODORO: I feel ashamed. The dream's over.
The only thing left now's oblivion.

TRISTAN: Well, you'll really have to grovel
to get Marcela to take you back.

TEODORO: You think so? It won't take that long.

MARCELA comes in.

MARCELA: When life makes us one of love's pretenders,
the heart's tide surges, clings to love that's true
and as I struggle to forget, my heart surrenders,
yields itself up whole to memories of you.
There's no honour here, there's no hope of life,
and there's no remedy in this deceit;
I'll seek vengeance as another's wife
and take comfort there, my heart's death complete.

But as I say it, as I voice this cold plan,
I become the victim of my own retribution,
for I could never love another man
and piling pain upon pain brings no solution.
The heart's an ocean. It'll not subside
I am my heart. There's nowhere else to hide.

TEODORO: Marcela!

MARCELA: Who's that?

TEODORO: Teodoro.
Have you forgotten me so soon?

MARCELA: I've forgotten you so completely
I've even forgotten myself.
If I am myself, I see you,
I imagine you, and it hurts,
and although my heart clings to you,
I banish it, send it elsewhere.
How dare you even speak my name?
How does it not turn to poison
on your treacherous lips?

TEODORO: I tested you,
and you failed. I have been informed
that your eyes have wandered already,
that someone else has filled my shoes.

MARCELA: You don't throw stones at a window
to test the quality of the glass.
I don't believe a word of it.
Teodoro, how well I know you.
It was *your* eyes that had wandered,
dazzled by the promise of gold.
So how's it going? Not like you thought?
Not such a glittering reward?
Your heavenly love not so divine?
What's gone wrong? And what's wrong with you?
Has the whirlwind changed direction
and you've come back down to earth for me?
Or is this just another test?

I tell you this: I'll be delighted,
Teodoro, if you've come here
to wish my new love and me
every joy for our wedding day.

TEODORO: Revenge is sweet. I understand.
But it is not a noble thing.
Real love's born from humility.
Marcela: I'm yours. You've won.
I admit I was fanciful,
the victim of a fantasy,
and if I've hurt you, my darling,
then forgive me; it's in your heart.
And it's for your heart I've come back,
not because my dreams are beyond me,
not because my folly lacked reason.
but because of my memories.
And those memories will awaken yours
safe in the knowledge that you've won.

MARCELA: No, God forbid I distract you
when your dreams are within your grasp.
You're making progress; persevere
or your mistress will think you a coward.
Follow your heart; I'm following mine.
If I love Fabio, where's the wrong,
since you had left me already?
It's not deceit; it's a good cure,
and although I've done no better,
as you say, the revenge is sweet.
God be with you; I've had enough
of your dreams, your hopes, your prattle…
Fabio shouldn't see us together,
because we're more than almost married.

She makes to leave.

TEODORO: Tristan, do something!

TRISTAN: Wait!

75

MARCELA: What?

TRISTAN: Think!

MARCELA: About what?

TRISTAN: Amends!
He's making them. And he's come back.
Just because he loves you again,
doesn't mean he stopped loving you.
He's the one who's come looking for you.
If he hurt you, that makes up for it.

DIANA and ANARDA appear.

DIANA: Teodoro! With Marcela!

ANARDA: You seem put out.

DIANA: They haven't seen us.
Quickly, let's hide behind that screen.

MARCELA: Tristan, let me go.

ANARDA: They've quarrelled.
Tristan's acting the peace-maker.

DIANA: The pimp more like...he drives me mad.

TRISTAN: A flash of lightning, a will o'the wisp
that's all she was; she's all show.
Nothing more than a pretty face...
He was dazzled for a moment,
but he scorns her and her riches now,
because he has a greater treasure
in you. It was a soap bubble.
And now it's burst. (*To TEODORO.*) Come over
       here.

DIANA: He makes a good go-between.

TEODORO: What for? She loves Fabio now.
Didn't she say that? She loves him?

TRISTAN: Now you're doing it.

TEODORO: It's for the best.
She can marry him, if she wants.

TRISTAN: Teodoro, get off your high horse.
Give me your hand and I'll fetch hers.

TEODORO: If you think I will, you're a fool.

TRISTAN: Marcela, please give yours to him...

TEODORO: When did I ever say to her
that I was in love with anyone?
Because she said she loved...someone.

TRISTAN: She didn't mean it...she was hurt.

MARCELA: I did mean it... I wasn't hurt.

TRISTAN: You keep out of it. Come on now,
both of you, you're being pig-headed.

TEODORO: I'll be damned if I try again.

MARCELA: I'll be damned if I give him my hand.

TRISTAN: No need to swear.

MARCELA: (*Aside, to TRISTAN.*) I'm not angry.
I'm really upset.

TRISTAN: (*Aside, to MARCELA.*) Keep going.
You're doing well.

DIANA: Clever little toad!

MARCELA: Let me go, Tristan. I've things to do.

TEODORO: Let her go, Tristan, I don't care.

TRISTAN: Off you go.

TEODORO: Stop her!

MARCELA: I can't go.

TRISTAN: I'm not stopping either of you.

MARCELA: I can't move.

TEODORO: No rock in the sea
could stand firmer here than me.

MARCELA: Come to my arms.

TEODORO: And you to mine.

TRISTAN: You didn't need me at all, did you?

ANARDA: This is what you waited to watch?

DIANA: It shows how little you can trust
a man and a woman.

TEODORO: You've been cruel.

TRISTAN: You'll both think that love found its way.
And I'll have lost my commission.

MARCELA: If I ever swapped you for Fabio,
or anyone else in the world,
then God grant you strike me dead.

TEODORO: And if I ever prove untrue,
then God grant you marry Fabio
as my eternal punishment.

MARCELA: You must right the wrong you did me.

TEODORO: It would not be right not to.
There's nothing I'd not do for you,
and nothing I'd not do with you.

MARCELA: Say: every other woman's ugly.

TEODORO: Absolute dogs. That was easy,
so great's my love.

MARCELA: I'm still jealous.
There's one more little thing I'd like.
But perhaps not in front of Tristan.

TRISTAN: Look, you've ignored me up to now.

MARCELA: Tell me that Diana's ugly.

TEODORO: Diana's ugly.

MARCELA: How ugly?

TEODORO: As the devil. Like a skunkrat.

MARCELA: And stupid?

TEODORO: Intolerably.

MARCELA: And doesn't she just rabbit on?

TEODORO: She rabbits and looks like a rabbit.

DIANA: I'll have to put a stop to this.
                 I am livid. I am burning.

ANARDA: No, my lady, let them blether.

TRISTAN: When it comes to badmouthing the countess,
                 I've a mouth on me like a foghorn.
                 First of all…

DIANA emerges.

DIANA: And second, Tristan?

MARCELA: My lady, I was just leaving!

MARCELA leaves, with a curtsy.

TRISTAN: The Countess?

TEODORO: The Countess!

DIANA: Teodoro!

TEODORO: My lady!

TRISTAN: There's a storm brewing,
                 I'll not wait to be hit by lightning.

TRISTAN leaves.

DIANA: Anarda, bring a writing desk.
                 Teodoro's going to take dictation.

TEODORO: My heart's pounding. What if she heard?

DIANA: To think he'd spurn me…for that thing!
                 What does she have that I don't,
                 and in abundance? But he wants her,
                 over me. They were laughing at me!

TEODORO: She's muttering away to herself.
                 Oh God, it's what I always said:
                 tapestries have ears, walls have tongues.

ANARDA returns with a small writing desk and a box of papers and pens.

ANARDA: I've brought this one, and your writing things.

DIANA: Come here, Teodoro. Take your pen.

TEODORO: She's making me write my own sentence.
Exile...execution, maybe.

He kneels at the little desk.

DIANA: Ready?

TEODORO: Ready.

DIANA: You're not comfortable.
Anarda, bring him a cushion.

TEODORO: I'm fine. Really I am.

DIANA: A cushion,
I said, Anarda. Put it there.

TEODORO: It's not my knees she's worried about.
She wants it to catch my head.

DIANA: Ready?

TEODORO: I'm signing the cross on the letter.
To keep the letter safe from harm.
I'll just do a few thousand more;
to keep me safe.

DIANA: It won't get lost.

She sits in a tall chair and dictates to him.

When a lady of great standing
declares herself to a common man,
if he should even look askance
at another, then he is vile,
lower than the low, a reptile.
And only a fool, the worst fool,
turns his back when fortune smiles at him.

TEODORO: Is that all?

DIANA: Isn't that enough?
Roll the paper up, Teodoro.

ANARDA: What are you doing, my lady?

DIANA: I'm making a fool of myself.
            For love.

ANARDA: Who are you in love with?

DIANA: Stop pretending you don't know.
            Even the walls are whispering his name.

TEODORO: The paper's rolled. What name should I put?

DIANA: Put your own name, Teodoro.
            Keep it; maybe you'll understand
            if you read it at your leisure.

She leaves.

TEODORO: I have no idea what's going on.
            This woman's like some mad doctor,
            bleeding me every now and then,
            watching as my veins pump out blood
            and then staunching the flow with ice.
            This is love by a thousand cuts.
            God knows whether it's kill or cure.

MARCELA returns.

MARCELA: What did she say? I couldn't hear.

TEODORO: I had to write a promissory note.
            Requesting money for your dowry.
            She's going to marry you. To Fabio.

MARCELA: What?

TEODORO: I wish you both every joy,
            and from now on I entreat you
            never to speak my name again,
            even in jest.

MARCELA: What's happening?

TEODORO: It's happened.

He leaves.

MARCELA: I don't believe this.
It's that mad woman.
Just one smile from her
and he starts spinning,
like an empty bucket
on her water-wheel.
When he's on the ground
she fills him to the brim
with her favours,
hoists him to the top
and empties him again.
It's me who suffers
while you go running
to her crooked finger.
She smiles and you go,
and when she has you
in the palm of her hand
she'll drop you again.
And back you'll crawl.
How can I bear this?

The Marquis RICARDO and FABIO appear.

RICARDO: I came, Fabio, *toute de suite* for my sweet.
                I shall not rest until I've kissed her hands

FABIO: Marcela, please, fetch my lady.
             Tell her the Marquis has arrived.

MARCELA: Jealousy, you've become a tyrant.
             What do you want of me now?

FABIO: Marcela…

MARCELA: I'm going.

FABIO: And tell her
             her husband, our new lord, is here.

MARCELA leaves.

RICARDO: Come to my lodgings tomorrow,
             and you will have one thousand crowns.

> And…one of the best stud stallions
> Naples ever saw!

FABIO: One thousand!
> I mean such generosity
> is not deserved. But well received,
> nonetheless.

RICARDO: And there will be more.
> Though you are my lady's servant,
> I count you as my dearest friend.

FABIO: I kiss your feet.

RICARDO: Pray, pray, my friend,
> trifling tokens of gratitude.
> And there will be much more to come.

DIANA enters.

DIANA: Marquis, what a surprise.

RICARDO: Hardly a surprise,
> after Fabio delivered your message.
> So much rejection weighs down the spirit,
> and when these gladdest of tidings reached me,
> that I, your devoted slave, am your chosen one,
> then wild beasts in a cordon round your door
> would not have stopped me from coming here
>   now
> to kneel before you and kiss your tiny feet.

He kneels.

> My joy is such that mere madness is not enough.
> I am constrained to take madness to new heights,
> for when did I think in my wildest thoughts
> that my fond hopes, my dreaming desires
> would ever be anything more than that?

DIANA: I am at a loss to answer.
> I sent for you? Is this some jest?

RICARDO: What's going on, Fabio?

FABIO: Good sir,
         I brought you here with good reason.
         It was Teodoro who told me.

DIANA: Teodoro's too quick off the mark.
         He must have heard me yesterday,
         comparing you to Federico,
         who, 'in spite of being my cousin,
         pales in his dazzling reflection',
         I said. He's leapt to conclusions.
         I beg you, sir, forgive these fools.

RICARDO: Your holy image gives this man sanctuary
         I kiss your feet in gratitude and withdraw,
         hoping my constancy one day will prevail.

RICARDO leaves.

DIANA: Imbecile, are you happy now?

FABIO: Me? Why blame me, my lady?

DIANA: Bring Teodoro.

As FABIO leaves.

                    God, he was quick.
         He must have sprinted round,
         the pompous fool.

FABIO: A thousand crowns.
         Five years to earn that. And a horse...

DIANA: What now, love? What test have you in store?
         I'd put him from my mind. What new surprise,
         what trap, will you spring? Is there still more?
         'It's not me, it's my shadow', love replies.
         So you, jealousy, do you still protest?
         Your angry voice is hissing in my head,
         giving me counsel and judgment so grotesque
         that if I paid heed, my honour'd soon be dead.
         Love and jealousy, you rip my soul apart.
         I love a man. I love a man completely,
         and if I could I'd sail out towards his heart.

But I must remember who I am: I am the sea.
If honour doesn't abate the storm, the wind die
    down
then I fear that the sea itself may well drown.

TEODORO and FABIO enter.

FABIO: He threatened to kill me on the spot.
              I miss the money though.

TEODORO: Listen,
              let me give you a piece of advice.

FABIO: Go on.

TEODORO: The Count's climbing the walls,
              thinking he's lost out to his rival.
              Go and tell him the wedding's off,
              and he'll give you your thousand crowns.

FABIO: Good advice.

TEODORO: Good man.

FABIO leaves.

                        Thank God.
              You sent for me.

DIANA: Indeed I did.
              I thought that dolt would never go.

TEODORO: I have been…em…meditating
              for a long hour on your letter.
              And, please forgive me if I'm wrong,
              I think I understand its…meaning.
              I see now that my…hesitation
              was a function of the…respect,
              the great respect, I have for you.
              But…to hide behind this barrier,
              in the face of your persuasion,
              was excessively respectful.
              Foolishly so. With all respect,
              therefore, I love you. With respect,
              because love rests upon respect.

I hope that I am making sense,
because I feel rather...on edge.

DIANA: I believe you, Teodoro.
Such love's in the natural order.
I'm your lady; you're my servant.
Indeed, as the one I most favour
among all the servants of this house,
I would expect you to love me.

TEODORO: I don't understand this language.

DIANA: There is nothing to understand,
no reason to let your thoughts wander
an inch beyond this line between us.
Curb your desire. Let me be frank.
Your merits are so scant, so poor,
that the slightest sign of favour
from a lady of noble birth
should keep you happy all your days.

TEODORO: My lady, if I may make so bold,
is a lady of intelligence,
whose wit and perception enjoy
many moments of lucidity.
But, once again if I may ask,
why give me hopes as you have done,
so many hopes that made my mind reel
and left me feeling exhausted
so that I was ill for a month
and came close to breaking down.
When I'm cold, you turn to fire,
and when I burn, you turn to ice.
Leave me alone, with Marcela.
Don't be a dog in a manger,
too jealous to let me marry,
too honourable to marry me.
Eat, if that's what you want to do,
or else let others eat in peace.
I can't survive on your diet

of tattered hopes and shattered dreams.
Otherwise, just let me return
to where I love, and be loved back.

DIANA: I warn you: you'll not turn to her.
Have any other one you want.
But not Marcela.

TEODORO: Why not her?
Marcela loves me, I love her,
and you say, go and look elsewhere!
I have to have somebody else
when there's no one else that I want?
I adore her; she adores me.
Our love is real. And down to earth.

DIANA: Insolent wretch. I'll have you killed.

She strikes him.

TEODORO: My lady!

DIANA: That's for Marcela!
And that's for the line you've just crossed,
you crude, vile liar, you cheat!

FABIO and Count FEDERICO enter.

FABIO: We should leave.

FEDERICO: Absolutely right,
Fabio, we should. But we won't.
My dear cousin, what's going on?

DIANA: Putting a servant in his place.

FEDERICO: And may I be of assistance?

DIANA: By not meddling in my business.

FEDERICO: I'll call at some other moment,
perhaps when you are more relaxed.

DIANA: I'm pleased to see you Federico.
This was a tiny storm at sea.
Do come inside; we have to talk.

It's time I made my purpose clear
on the subject of the Marquis.

DIANA leaves.

FEDERICO: Fabio!

FABIO: My lord?

FEDERICO: What's going on?
There's more to this than meets the eye.
Such violent dislike usually
conceals some liking, no less violent.

FABIO: I swear, my lord, I've no idea.
I've never seen her behave like that.

FEDERICO: Well, she doesn't pull her punches.
She's drawn blood.

They leave. TEODORO mops himself with his handkerchief.

TEODORO: If this isn't love, what name can we give it?
Such madness is surely part of love's excess,
and if this passion's the way such ladies live it,
then they're furies, and that, a furious caress.
Their honour puts them on a different plane,
while lesser lovers may give and take,
and, where there's simple joy, instead gives pain,
and brings sweet destruction in love's wake.
Her hand has the power to strike and to beat,
but the power of love has a scope much wider,
and punishment from such a hand tasted sweet
when I felt that fire raging deep inside her.
A fire and a rage beyond all normal measure,
so that when she struck me, we both felt pleasure.

TRISTAN enters.

TRISTAN: That's me all over: late again,
missing all the fun, like a virgin
at an orgy.

TEODORO: Tristan.

TRISTAN: There's blood...
          on your handkerchief.

TEODORO: Yes, there's blood.
          It's love's lesson in jealousy.

TRISTAN: My God, love's a vicious teacher.

TEODORO: Don't look so shocked. She's mad, that's all.
           It's her passion, her mad desire.
           She looks at my face and wants me,
           but my face's the living mirror
           of her dishonour. So she hits it.
           It's quite simple really.

TRISTAN: Maybe.
           Say fat Paca or big Juana
           had a go at me, tooth and nails,
           tearing my shirt, ripping my skin,
           because I've been playing around,
           well, you can sort of understand.
           They're great big clods of working girls,
           who wear knitted stockings and clogs.
           They're just peasants. But a lady...
           Where's her self-respect? Her control?
           You should be very careful, sir.

TEODORO: I don't know what to think, Tristan.
           She loves me and then she hates me.
           She doesn't want me for her own,
           but won't let me be Marcela's.
           I turn away, she makes me look.
           I say nothing, she makes me speak.
           She's neither one thing or the other.
           If she can't eat, nobody will.

TRISTAN: There was once this learned doctor –
           a professor, teacher, you know.
           His housekeeper and his butler
           were the very bane of his life,
           fighting and quarrelling all day long.
           They shouted through lunch, through dinner,

even kept him awake at night.
He couldn't study, couldn't think,
for the racket they were kicking up.
He came home early from class one day,
and went straight up to his bedroom,
where he found them snug in his bed,
kissing and cuddling. What did he say?
'Great! You've made up. No more shouting!'
Maybe you'll both make up as well.

DIANA comes in.

DIANA: Teodoro.

TEODORO: My lady.

TRISTAN: My God,
can she see though walls?

DIANA: I wondered
how you are; I came to see you.

TEODORO: You can see how I am.

DIANA: Are you well?

TEODORO: I am well.

DIANA: But not 'well, thank you'?
Not 'well, at your service'?

TEODORO: Hardly.
I'm not keen on being in your service,
if it means this sort of treatment.

DIANA: How little you know.

TEODORO: What can I know?
I feel but I don't understand.
I don't understand what you say,
but I feel your anger and your blows.
Your anger, when I don't love you,
and your blows, when I say I do.
I forget you: you write to me.
I come to you: you take offence.

You try to make me understand,
and when I do, you say I'm a fool.
Kill me, give me life, call a truce
between these extremes.

DIANA: I made you bleed?

TEODORO: Yes.

DIANA: Show me your handkerchief.

TEODORO: What for?

DIANA: I want to see your blood.
Give me your handkerchief.

She keeps the handkerchief.

                                                  Now go.
Octavio has money for you.
Two thousand crowns.

TEODORO: Two thousand crowns!
What for?

DIANA: To buy more handkerchiefs.

She leaves.

TEODORO: This has passed all understanding.

TRISTAN: I can't make head or tail of it.
It might be witchcraft.

TEODORO: Two thousand crowns!

TRISTAN: It's good work, if you can get it.
Being hit.

TEODORO: For handkerchiefs, she said.
And then she kept the bloodied one.

TRISTAN: It's proof your nose is a virgin.
She's had her wicked way with it,
now she's paying for the pleasure.
You should make her pay: through the nose.

TEODORO: She may be a dog in a manger,
           but when she bites, she licks you better.

TRISTAN: These extremes will resolve themselves,
           like the doctor's servants: in bed.

TEODORO: God willing, Tristan, God willing.

ACT THREE

FEDERICO and RICARDO appear.

RICARDO: You saw her?

FEDERICO: Yes.

RICARDO: Actually strike him?

FEDERICO: For a lady of her standing
to strike a man in the face,
well, let's say it doesn't quite add up.
And he's been swaggering about
the place lately like a peacock.

RICARDO: She's a woman…but he's a servant.

FEDERICO: Heading for trouble, both of them.

RICARDO: It's the fable of the two pots.
Two pots: one clay, the other copper,
swept away by a river in flood.
The clay one chose to keep its distance,
frightened a clash would shatter it.
This man and this woman are pots.
He's made from clay, but she's wrought iron,
and believe you me, he'll smash
if he goes anywhere near here.

FEDERICO: Perhaps I didn't see what I saw.
But he dresses like a gentleman now,
with horses and servants galore.
Diana's given her peacock wings.
He has all the trappings of favour.

RICARDO: Such ostentation comes at a price.
If we choose to stand idly by,
all Naples will be whispering.
It is an offence to your name.
It brings dishonour to your family.
Whether it's true or not, he dies.

FEDERICO: He must. We've no choice. But how?

RICARDO: Naples isn't short of cut-throats,
vermin who'd kill their mothers for gold.
Blood for money. A simple trade.
All we have to do is find one.

FEDERICO: I beg you then, do it quickly!

RICARDO: We shall punish his impudence.
We'll do it today.

FEDERICO: Those men coming…
are they cut-throats?

RICARDO: Absolutely.

FEDERICO: Then the heavens are on our side.

FURIO, ANTONELO and LIRANO, all lackeys, appear, accompanied by TRISTAN, who is ostentatiously wearing new clothes.

FURIO: You've done very well for yourself.
Spread a bit of the good luck round.
Get the wine in.

ANTONELO: Tristan's the gent.

TRISTAN: I am and *noblesse* doth *oblige.*

LIRANO: Great suit.

TRISTAN: Ha! This suit's an old rag
in comparison to what's coming.
I've all my skittles in a row
and if things work out as they should,
I shall be the secretary's
secretary.

LIRANO: Well, the Countess
has set her glad eye on your boss.

TRISTAN: He's her right-hand man, the doorway
to her favour.

ANTONELO: Talking of right hands,
mine needs a drink in it. Let's go.

FURIO: There's a tavernacle right here.
Let's go in and take communion.

TRISTAN: A few bottles of good Greek wine.
I feel like speaking a bit of Greek
and after a couple of bottles,
everything sounds Greek to me.

RICARDO: The pale-skinned one, he's the leader.
The rest of them all respect him.
There's an evil glint in his eye.
Celio!

CELIO runs on.

CELIO: My lord?

RICARDO: Those gentlemen.
Ask the pale one to come over.

CELIO: Good sir, can you spare a moment
to have a word with my master,
before entering this holy shrine?

TRISTAN: You must excuse me, my good friends.
Some wandering prince requires my help.
Go and try a few casks of wine,
and get some feta and vine leaves
– I love Greek food – while I sort this out.

ANTONELO: Just be quick.

TRISTAN: Speed's my middle name.
Sir, your underling requested
the pleasure of my company.

RICARDO: Seeing you with your fearless friends
has made Count Federico and I
wonder just how fearless you are.
Could you kill a man, for instance?

TRISTAN: I know these men. I'll play along.

FEDERICO: Answer him.

TRISTAN: Sirs, you speak in jest
Just as my strength comes from him above,
I swear in the whole of Naples
there's not a sword doesn't tremble
at my name. You've heard of Hector.
Well, forget him. There is no Hector
where I raise *my* sword in anger.
Italy's most prolific killer.
That's me.

FEDERICO: This is the man we need.
We intended no disrespect.
Indeed, quite the reverse is true.
We admire your...brutal honesty.
So if you would kill a man for us,
we will see you well rewarded.

TRISTAN: The usual price: two hundred crowns,
and I'll kill the devil himself.

RICARDO: Do it tonight and we'll make it three.

TRISTAN: I need his name. And half up front.

RICARDO: You know Diana, Countess of Belflor?

TRISTAN: I have friends who serve in her house.

RICARDO: Could you kill one of her servants?

TRISTAN: Bring them all on: men servants, maids.
I'll slit her horses' throats, if you want.

RICARDO: His name's Teodoro.

TRISTAN: Oh him?
Then there is a difficulty.
Teodoro never stirs at night.
He skulks at home, because he knows
he's caused offence to gents like yourselves.
There's another way to do it.
I've been asked to be his servant.
I'll accept, and then one dark night,
soon, I'll slit him from arse to nose.
Rest in peace. In fact, in pieces.

No one'll be any the wiser.
What do you think of that for a plan?

FEDERICO: Heaven's door opened when we found you.
There's not a better man in Naples.
Once you've got his trust, kill him.
Then report back.

TRISTAN: A half up front...

RICARDO: Take this, there's fifty in this purse.
When you're in and won his trust,
you'll get another fifty crowns.
And when the job's done, the full price.

TRISTAN: We have a contract. I must go.
Knuckler, Bruiser and Ironfist
are waiting for me inside there.
Or else, they'll know something's cooking,
and they'll want to dip their bread in too.

RICARDO: Very wise.

They walk away from TRISTAN. As they leave.

He's a professional!
Teodoro's as good as dead.

FEDERICO: I'd hate to meet him on a dark night.

TRISTAN goes towards the tavern, thinks better of it and starts to run.

TRISTAN: I ought to warn Teodoro.
The wine can wait. That's him coming now!

TEODORO enters.

Where are you off to, sir?

TEODORO: Tristan,
I've no idea where I'm going,
I'm wandering, I don't know why,
just wandering aimlessly
following just one single thought;
dare I lift my eyes to the sun?

97

Yesterday we talked for hours,
but today her eyes are stone cold.
You'd swear she'd never seen me before
or knew my name. She's doing it
to discredit me, make me a fool
in Marcela's eyes.

TRISTAN: Listen, sir.
We can't be seen out together.
Let's go home.

TEODORO: Why?

TRISTAN: Listen to me.
This is how we're going to save your life.

TEODORO: My life?

TRISTAN: Keep your voice down, for God's sake.
Listen: here's what we're going to do.
Ricardo and Federico paid me,
just now, a fortune, to kill you.

TEODORO: They want you to kill me! Why?

TRISTAN: They saw the Countess hitting you,
and put two and two together.
They took me for some ruffian
and contracted me on the spot.
Two hundred crowns, fifty up front.
I told them I could win your trust,
by entering into your service.
That's how I'd get the chance to kill you.
Not that I would.

TEODORO: I wish to God
someone would put an end to this,
put me out of my misery.

TRISTAN: Are you mad?

TEODORO: How could I not be?
I'm so near and yet still so far,
and I'm burning up. Trust me,

if Diana found any way,
she'd marry me. Without thinking.

Pause.

TRISTAN: What if I found a way? What then?

TEODORO: I'd say you could out-scheme Ulysses.

TRISTAN: What if I schemed you a father?
A noble father. Would that work?

TEODORO: Yes...

TRISTAN: Count Ludovico lost his son,
about twenty years ago now.
The thing is – he was called Teodoro.
He was at sea, en route to Malta.
where his uncle was Grand Master,
when his ship was taken by Turks.
His father waited for a ransom,
but nothing more was ever heard.
He's the father, you're the son.
Long lost, back from a watery grave.
Leave it with me.

TEODORO: What are you doing?
Tristan, stay well away from this.
It's becoming too dangerous.

TRISTAN: Look we're home. You go in and rest.
Trust me. She'll be yours tomorrow.

TRISTAN leaves.

TEODORO: That's not the remedy I'll seek to find
to so much pain, more pain that I can bear,
for love knows that lovers are resigned
when the occasion is no longer there.
So I'll put earth between us, and soften
the lightning fierceness of your raging heart,
and let earth quell the pain that so often
struck, and threatened to tear my soul apart.
Earth where things begin and have their end,

cold distance where warm memories expire.
So many have learned how dark earth may mend
the wounds of love, and douse its burning fire.
Dust to dust, and ashes where love has been.
Memories lie buried, in the earth between.

DIANA appears.

DIANA: Are you in better spirits today?

TEODORO: My spirits are the measure
of my love, I'd not change them.
If they are my illness, I seek no cure.
This is a grief of such sweetness
that even though death may draw near
I cannot mourn my destruction.
But there is something that weighs heavy,
a reason that compels me now
to remove my illness from its cause.

DIANA: You want to leave?

TEODORO: I have to leave.
They intend to have me killed.

DIANA: So,
you want to die, but not be killed?

TEODORO: Die for you...not be killed uselessly.
They envy me, although God knows
they don't know what they're envying.
It's certainly no longer joy.
That's why I beg your permission
to let me sail at once for Spain.

DIANA: That would be a...noble solution.
Though I'll weep at your departure,
removing the occasion of sin
will bring you peace; and honour to my house.
Since the day he saw me strike you,
Federico's been suspicious.
He's asked me time and again
to have you thrown onto the street.

Go to Spain. I'll make arrangements
for you to have six thousand crowns.

TEODORO: Your enemies will be silenced
by my departure. I kiss your feet.

DIANA: I'm made of flesh and blood...please go.
I can't bear this.

TEODORO moves away.

TEODORO: She's weeping, but what can I do?

DIANA: So you're leaving?

TEODORO: I am, my lady.

DIANA: Safe journey. Wait!

TEODORO: My lady?

DIANA: Nothing.
Go.

TEODORO: I'm going.

DIANA: This is torture.
You're still here?

TEODORO: I'm going, my lady.

TEODORO leaves.

DIANA: The door's slammed; he's gone,
and I'm left alone.
So damn you honour,
and damn your harsh laws.
You're some men's fiction
to keep life at bay,
to deny desire.
Damn you and damn them
for thinking you up.
But without you, what then?
this world's in chaos,
and only honour
keeps us where we are,
maintains life's balance.

TEODORO returns.

TEODORO: Forgive me. I wanted to be sure
I have your leave to go today.

DIANA: I don't know...and nor can you know
how much seeing you here again
causes me the most bitter pain,
or else you'd not have returned.

TEODORO: I've returned in search of myself,
because I find myself nowhere,
and like a judge returns a corpse
to a grieving family, bereft,
I beg you, release me. Give me back.

DIANA: Tell me, how can I release you
if you keep coming back to me?
Love's in such dispute with my honour
that your presence will make me stumble.
Go, Teodoro; don't ask any more.
Though part of you will always stay,
just as part of me goes with you.

TEODORO: God be with you, your ladyship.

TEODORO leaves.

DIANA: Your ladyship's lost me everything.
Damn my lady. I'd have been his
were it not for her. And he's gone.
The man who brought light to these eyes.
So let them suffer,
eyes that saw wrong.
Let them weep long.
My eyes, you are to blame for this,
for casting your gaze down so low,
and seeing love there was seeing wrong.
Do not weep, for tears bring relief.
So let them suffer,
eyes that saw wrong.
Let them weep long.

The looking's innocent enough,
they'll say; if the sun shines on mud
there's no mud will stick to the sun.
Stop weeping, my eyes, you've no cause for tears.

MARCELA comes in.

MARCELA: My lady, may I speak to you?
I've served you now for many years,
faithfully and with diligence,
and I presume on that service
to say that it's now in your power
to resolve my situation,
and indeed yours, if, as I think,
you'd prefer not to see me again.

DIANA: What exactly is in my power?

MARCELA: Teodoro is leaving for Spain,
I hear, fearing his life's in danger.
If you sent me with him, as his wife,
you'd never set eyes on me again.

DIANA: Are you sure that it's what he wants?

MARCELA: Would I ask you if it wasn't?

DIANA: You've spoken to him?

MARCELA: We've spoken.
It's exactly what he asked me.

DIANA: More agony…and at this time.

MARCELA: We've talked it over together.

DIANA: Unreasoning honour, forgive me,
for love's about to lose control.
No, wait: this is easily solved.

MARCELA: My lady? Why won't you answer?

DIANA: I'm sorry, Marcela, but no.
I need you here. What you suggest
offends the love I have for you.
And Fabio, you know, adores you.

I shall marry you to Fabio.
Let Teodoro depart alone.

MARCELA: I hate Fabio! I love Teodoro!

DIANA: I could reply so easily.
I love him too! One single lapse,
and the truth like the sea comes flooding in.
Fabio's better suited to you.

MARCELA: My lady...

DIANA: I will hear no more!

DIANA leaves.

MARCELA: Then why strive for that which cannot be,
knowing that I am hers to command,
why stand in the face of jealousy,
when my whole life's held within her hand?
Then turn back, my steps, on the way you've
taken.
What else can be done? The day is lost,
But there's a death in every love forsaken,
every love left standing like a tree in frost.
The beauty of its flowers, its colours and scent,
blighted by her rancorous cold in late spring,
they're gone now, the tree dead, all life spent.
Nothing's grown, nothing lives on...nothing...
What good was there in the brightest flower
when the tree's dead, and the earth turned sour?

*MARCELA leaves. Count LUDOVICO, an old man, enters,
with CAMILO.*

CAMILO: I know that this is delicate.
Your estate must be safeguarded,
and the only way's through an heir.

LUDOVICO: The years, young man, are not our friends,
and with every year that passes,
I grow less inclined to re-marry.
Caution, I think, is the better judge.
What if I were to take a wife

and not father a son? What then?
I'd still be married, and an old man
doesn't lie easy with a young wife,
like green ivy clinging to an elm
so while he withers, his wife thrives.
I had a son and I lost him.
And not one day has gone by
without me thinking about him.
He might be alive and married.
Or he might be dead and long gone.

A PAGE enters.

PAGE: You have a visitor, my lord.
               A Greek merchant.

LUDOVICO: A Greek merchant!
              What business does he have with me?
              Show him in, I suppose.

The PAGE leaves and returns with TRISTAN, dressed as an Armenian and wearing an outlandish turban. He is accompanied by FURIO, similarly attired.

TRISTAN: Your grace,
              that you receive a foreigner
              to your home does you and Naples proud.
              The Lord will reward such kindness,
              and will bring you your heart's desire.

LUDOVICO: Any Christian is welcome here.
              You are far from home. How can I help?

TRISTAN: I sailed from Constantinople,
              and from there onward to Cyprus,
              before tacking north to Venice,
              laden with spices and carpets.
              I left my crew there to unload
              and travelled by land to Naples,
              a city I was keen to see.
              It is indeed a great city.

LUDOVICO: A great city, yes.

TRISTAN: Yes, indeed,
Let me unravel my reasons
for coming to this…em…great place.
I shall lay them out before you
like one of my Persian carpets…
My father was a Greek merchant,
just as I'm a merchant…and Greek.
He bartered – shamefully – in slaves.
One day in Papadopolous,
in the market, he bought a boy,
the most beautiful child you've seen,
a child any father'd adore,
from Turkish traders who'd snatched him
from a galley bound for Malta.

LUDOVICO: Camilo, my heart is trembling.

TRISTAN: My father took a shine to the boy,
and brought him back home to Armenia.
Did I mention we're from Armenia?
And there he lived with my family,
as a brother to my sister and me.

LUDOVICO: Wait, friend, your words are like daggers.

TRISTAN: Taking it hook, line and sinker.

LUDOVICO: Sir, this boy…did he tell you his name?

TRISTAN: Teodoro.

LUDOVICO: Teodoro!
Camilo, I can't contain my tears.

TRISTAN: But wait- the story now thickens.
Sue Valaki – my sister, sir,
took more than a shine to this boy,
so beautiful was he, so well-turned,
that in my father's absence,
and he barely sixteen years old,
what was bound to happen, happened,
She began to show, he panicked
and fled, leaving us all grief-stricken.

My father Hugh Muss Kababolous
– did I mention that was his name? –
my dad cared less for her disgrace
than for the loss of Teodoro.
He died heart-broken just after.
We called the child Terry Massalata,
and he lives to this very day
in…the capital of Armenia.
So we come to the final chapter.
This very morning, in my inn,
I was recounting the story
to a Greek girl who serves breakfast.
'Have you heard of Count Ludovico',
she said, in Greek. 'He might be his.'
I was astounded, and resolved
to come and see you straightaway.
But now! The final twist!
You know the Countess of Belflor?
Well, I had business in her house,
and called by there on my way here.
You'll never guess who opened the door.
Teodoro!

LUDOVICO: Teodoro! He's here?

TRISTAN: He'd have run away if he could,
so deeply ashamed does he feel.
I recognised him instantly,
and I hugged him like a brother.
I held him, clutched him to my breast,
and we talked of days gone by.
But now I come to the climax.
He is employed by the Countess,
and was anxious she shouldn't know
of his shameful past as a slave.
'You are the son of a grandee
of this very city', I said.
'You have nothing to feel but pride.'
And so I came to see you to ask

if this man is in truth your son,
and let you know you've a grandson
and perhaps he could come to Naples,
because my sister would bring him,
not because she's desperate to marry,
not that she's not a pretty good catch,
but to let Terry Massalata
meet his illustrious granddad.

LUDOVICO: My heart tells me that this is true,
my great, great friend. Let me embrace you,
for you have brought me back to life.
Camilo, advise me. Tell me,
should I write or go straight to him?

CAMILO: You should follow what your heart says.
You've suffered long enough...why wait?

LUDOVICO: Then come with me, my trusted friend,
and you will make my joy complete.

TRISTAN: Ah, good sir, there's other business
to which I fear I must attend.
A small matter of some carpets,
not far from here. I shall return.
We shall go now. Peter.

CAMILO: Peter?

TRISTAN: Peterbread.

FURIO: Yes, master.

As they leave.

TRISTAN: A real strokopolous.

FURIO: Fantasticous.

TRISTAN: Let's make tracksious.

CAMILO: A strange musical language, Greek.

LUDOVICO: I'm ready, Camilo. Let's go.

LUDOVICO and CAMILO leave in another direction.

TRISTAN: Have they gone?

FURIO: The old boy's on wings.

TRISTAN: Imagine this was really true.

FURIO: It'd certainly be unexpected.

TRISTAN: Here, I want to get this nightdress off.
I don't want to be seen like this.

FURIO: Let me help you.

TRISTAN: It's amazing,
you know, that his love's still so strong.
Right that's us.

FURIO: Where'll I wait for you?

TRISTAN: The Cock and Bull.

FURIO: See you later.

FURIO goes.

TRISTAN: What's money when you've wits like mine?

He untucks his cloak, uncomfortably folded and knotted between his legs.

My God, that was uncomfortable.
I felt like some Venetian castrato.
All right, let's dump the fancy dress.

RICARDO and FEDERICO appear.

FEDERICO: That's him right there! The cut-throat
who was going to kill Teodoro.

RICARDO: Sir, is this the way your sort behave,
with all your easy promises?
Your reputation! What a farce!

TRISTAN: Look…

FEDERICO: Look! You are not our equal!
We pay you and you serve us, that's all,
Do you understand? Well, do you?

TRISTAN: I understand perfectly, my lords.
But, my good sirs, you condemn me
without hearing what I've achieved.
I'm in his service already,
and with this hand, by which I swear,
with this sledgehammer of blood and bone,
I shall fell him like an ox.
I shall paint his blood on the walls.
But sirs, prudence is a virtue,
greatly esteemed by the ancients.
And we must proceed with caution
so that your names and, my murdering skill,
do not come to public notice.
So, my lords, do *you* understand?
Trust me, sirs, he's dead on his feet.
I'm watching his every movement,
studying him by day and night,
taking notes, making calculations.
He's melancholic by day.
By night he locks himself away
with his obsessions. So trust me,
for I know exactly when to strike.

FEDERICO: You were right, he's a professional.

RICARDO: Teodoro's days are numbered.

FEDERICO: Not so loud.

TRISTAN: There is the matter
of the outstanding fifty crowns.
I have to buy a trusty steed,
to make my escape. For all our sakes.

RICARDO: Here. Kill Teodoro for us,
and there'll be more than cash in it.
If you follow my drift.

TRISTAN: I do.
Count on me. If you follow mine.
I take my leave of you. For now.
Best that we're not seen together.

FEDERICO: Very wise.

TRISTAN: You'll see just how wise.

TRISTAN leaves.

FEDERICO: Fine chap.

RICARDO: A real fox.

FEDERICO: He'll kill him.

RICARDO: Oh yes, slaughter him like a bull.

CELIO enters.

CELIO: You'll never believe what's happened.

FEDERICO: Where are you going? What *has* happened?

CELIO: It's the most astonishing news,
            though whether it's good news for you...
            Did you not see that crowd of people
            rushing to Count Ludovico's palace?

RICARDO: The old bugger's kicked the bucket, eh?

CELIO: My lord, I beg you: hear me out.
            They've gone to congratulate him.
            His son's come back, the one who was lost.

RICARDO: Heart warming. So what?

CELIO: Well, perhaps
            it may have some impact on your plans,
            on the personal plans both of you
            are pursuing with Countess Diana.
            His long lost son's Teodoro.

FEDERICO: He's Count Ludovico's son? Shit! Shit!

RICARDO: And how has all this come to light?

CELIO: It's quite a story, believe me.
            And each time it changes in the telling,
            and grows, so it's a real epic.
            You're hard pushed to keep up with it.

FEDERICO: This is a disaster. That's it.

RICARDO: And I thought the way had been cleared.

FEDERICO: Let's go and find out what happened.

RICARDO: My hopes gone...turned to dust...

CELIO: It's true.
You couldn't make up a thing like that.

They leave. TEODORO enters, in travelling clothes, accompanied by MARCELA.

MARCELA: So, Teodoro, you're leaving?

TEODORO: Because of you; the odds are stacked
much too high against us. That's why...

MARCELA: Your excuse is as false as ever.
You turned your back on me for her,
and now your dreams have fallen through,
you're left with nothing, but failure.

TEODORO: Her? Who are you talking about?

MARCELA: I'm talking about Diana.
How can you deny that it's her?
Your desire's there for all to see,
and it's turned you into a coward
and a rash fool; yes, a coward
because you've not dared go beyond
the respect that her rank demands,
and a rash fool, because you dreamed
that one day perhaps you might.
When can honour and love ever meet?
There are too many mountains,
too many icy slopes, in between.
Even as you leave, I still love you;
but at least I have my revenge,
and revenge helps us to forget.
That's love's way of keeping us intact.
If you think of me, then imagine
that I have forgotten you.
And you will feel desire cut through you,

into your flesh, like a sharp knife.
Men only want the impossible.

TEODORO: You've invented all this nonsense
because you're marrying Fabio.

MARCELA: Forced by your hand! By your contempt!

FABIO comes in.

FABIO: Teodoro! Ready for the road.
Enjoy your last moments with him,
Marcela.

TEODORO: Don't let your jealousy
get the better of you, Fabio.
It'll have a long way to travel.

FABIO: You're going?

TEODORO: What does it look like?

FABIO: The Countess wishes to see you.

DIANA appears, accompanied by DOROTEA and ANARDA.

DIANA: So, Teodoro, you're ready?

TEODORO: If my feet had wings, and not spurs,
my lady, I'd be in Spain by now.

DIANA: Are Teodoro's boxes all packed?

ANARDA: All packed, and waiting at the door.

FABIO: So, he's going?

MARCELA: You're still jealous?

DIANA: A quiet word.

TEODORO: I'm at your service.

TEODORO and DIANA draw aside.

DIANA: You're leaving.
And I love you.

TEODORO: I'm leaving
because of you and your cruelty.

DIANA: What else can I do?

TEODORO: You're crying.

DIANA: No... I've something in my eye.

TEODORO: It must be love.

DIANA: It must have been.
            A long time ago. It's out now.

TEODORO: I'm going, though the best of me stays.
            I leave my heart and soul with you.
            I've done no wrong in loving you;
            your beauty commands hearts and souls.
            As you command me. I am yours.

DIANA: This is misery.

TEODORO: My lady,
            I leave my heart and soul with you.

DIANA: You're crying.

TEODORO: No, my lady, I'm not.
            Like you, I've something in my eye.

DIANA: Tears are infectious.

TEODORO: They must have been.
            A long time ago. They're out now.

DIANA: One of your boxes... I filled it
            with some things...stupid, childish things...
            Forgive me, I couldn't help myself
            but I wanted you to have them
            If you open it to look at them,
            like the spoils of some great conquest,
            make sure you say: 'Diana
            put these here, with tears in her eyes'.

ANARDA: They're losing control.

DOROTEA: It's so hard.

ANARDA: We should stay, I think, for her sake,
            otherwise this could get much worse.
            Look...look...look...she's touching his hand.

DOROTEA: She doesn't know what she wants.
　　　　　The dog in the manger.

ANARDA: 　　　　　　　　　　It's too late.

DOROTEA: She should eat. Or let others eat.

Count LUDOVICO and CAMILO come in.

LUDOVICO: My dear Diana, forgive me
　　　　　for bursting into your home like this.
　　　　　Our acquaintance is limited,
　　　　　a source of constant regret for me,
　　　　　but my news won't brook formality.

DIANA: 　Count Ludovico…

LUDOVICO: 　　　　　　　Surely you've heard?
　　　　　The whole of Naples is agog.

DIANA: 　Heard?

LUDOVICO: 　　　　Everyone I saw stopped me.
　　　　　I thought I'd never get to see him.

DIANA: 　See who?

LUDOVICO: 　　　　My son!

DIANA: 　　　　　　　Your son!

LUDOVICO: 　　　　　　　　　You don't know?
　　　　　Have you never heard my story?
　　　　　How twenty years ago I sent
　　　　　my son, with his uncle to Malta,
　　　　　and his ship was taken by Turks?

DIANA: 　Count Ludovico, what's happened?

LUDOVICO: Fortune that played so bitter a trick
　　　　　has turned her smile on me at last.
　　　　　My son has been brought back to me!

DIANA: 　Thank you for bringing me the news.

LUDOVICO: You may bring me my son, in exchange.
　　　　　He's a servant in this household,
　　　　　with no knowledge of who he is.

If only his mother, God rest her,
were still alive...

DIANA: My servant? Fabio?

LUDOVICO: No, no, not Fabio. Teodoro!

DIANA: Teodoro!

LUDOVICO: Yes, Teodoro.

TEODORO: Me?

DIANA: Teodoro, is this true?

LUDOVICO: That's him?

TEODORO: My lord, I think that...

LUDOVICO: No, no buts.
           I have solid proof. Come to me,
           and let me hold you in my arms.

DIANA: Incredible.

ANARDA: Teodoro's
           really a Count, is he, my lady?

TEODORO: My lord...I can't think and daren't speak.
           I am in a state of deep shock.
           Am I really your son?

LUDOVICO: You are,
           and if there had been any doubt,
           seeing you would have dispelled it.
           I see in you the child you were.
           Come to my arms.

TEODORO: I'm not worthy
           to kiss your feet. Sir, I beg you...

LUDOVICO: You're the son I've always dreamed of.
           Let me look at you: such presence.
           Nobility's written in your face.
           Your birth and breeding are clearly
           etched on it. Come home with me now,
           where my estate will be your estate,
           come and repossess your coat of arms,
           the noblest in all of Naples.

TEODORO: Sir, I was leaving for Spain. I...

LUDOVICO: These arms of mine are Spain enough!

DIANA: My lord, may I offer a suggestion?
           Perhaps Teodoro should stay here,
           until he's gathered his thoughts.
           He's dressed more like a wayfarer
           than a gentleman of such good name.

LUDOVICO: You are quite right, of course. Thank you.
           There are so many people waiting.
           I must go and tell them the news.
           I ask one thing: before nightfall,
           let him come to me. To his home.

DIANA: You have my word.

LUDOVICO: Goodbye, Teodoro.
           My son.

TEODORO: I kiss your feet. My lord.

LUDOVICO: Camilo, were I to die now,
           I'd die happy.

CAMILO: He's a fine boy.
           I can see your spirit in him.

LUDOVICO: I'm terrified that I'll wake up.

*LUDOVICO and CAMILO leave. The other servants rush to
TEODORO.*

FABIO: Let us kiss your hands.

ANARDA: You're a lord;
           it would be a noble gesture.

DOROTEA: Grant your favour to us all, my lord.

MARCELA: The greatest lords *embrace* those they love.
           That's how they win their servants' hearts.

DIANA: Stand aside and stop your nonsense!
           Leave him alone! Lord Teodoro,
           now I ask you for *your* hand to kiss.

TEODORO:	And I in turn kneel at your feet, for truly now you are my lady.
DIANA:	Out, all of you!
MARCELA:	Well, Fabio?
FABIO:	I don't know what to make of it!
DOROTEA:	What do you think?
ANARDA:	The dog's had her day.
DOROTEA:	You mean she'll eat?
ANARDA:	Of course she will.
DOROTEA:	I hope she eats until she bursts.

The servants leave.

DIANA:	And Spain?
TEODORO:	Spain?
DIANA:	Remember saying: 'I'm going, though the best of me stays. I leave my heart and soul with you'?
TEODORO:	So now that fortune's on my side, you make fun.
DIANA:	You're so serious.
TEODORO:	We should remember our station, and treat each other with courtesy. As befits two equals.
DIANA:	You've changed.
TEODORO:	It seems to me your desire has changed. Your love's perverse, madam. I was your servant, you wanted me. But you cannot love an equal.
DIANA:	You're wrong; I'll marry you tonight.
TEODORO:	Then fortune has come full circle. There's nothing left for her to give.

DIANA: I am the happiest of women.
            I think you should go and get changed.

TEODORO: Yes, I have to inspect my estate.
            And go and see that father of mine.

DIANA: Farewell, my count.

TEODORO: Farewell, my countess.

DIANA: One thing...

TEODORO: What?

DIANA: 'What'? What do you mean?
            What way's that for a servant to talk!

TEODORO: The game has changed. I'm the master now.

DIANA: Don't give me cause to be jealous.
            Marcela won't like this at all.

TEODORO: She's a servant. No nobleman
            would stoop so low, to love a servant.

DIANA: I hope that you mean what you say.

TEODORO: You insult me.

DIANA: I insult you?
            And who am I to insult you?

TEODORO: My wife.

TEODORO leaves.

DIANA: I have everything I want.
            Hold firm, fortune, hold firm, hold firm.

RICARDO and FEDERICO appear.

RICARDO: Amidst all the celebration,
            we thought you'd like to share your news,
            with your friends.

DIANA: I'm delighted to.

FEDERICO: Your servant...is it true he's a lord?

DIANA: Forgive me, gentlemen, I must go.
            To see Count Teodoro. My husband.

She leaves.

RICARDO: This is dreadful!

FEDERICO: My brain's on fire!

RICARDO: If that dirty flea-ridden rogue
had killed him like he promised to...

TRISTAN appears.

FEDERICO: Speak of the devil. That's him now.

TRISTAN: Everything's falling into place.
Isn't it great, a lackey's wit
turns the whole of Naples upside down.

RICARDO: Hold on, whatever your name is.

TRISTAN: People call me Liquidator.
But Teodoro calls me Tristan.

FEDERICO: And have you...liquidated...him?

TRISTAN: I had the cleaver in my hand
when the walking corpse became a count.

RICARDO: So?

TRISTAN: We agreed three hundred crowns
to kill Teodoro the servant.
That's a bargain, a knock-down rate.
But to kill Teodoro the Count,
well, that's a very different thing.
Servants are half-dead already.
They're either starving or scheming,
obsessed with envy or daft with dreams.
I'm sorry: a Count costs four servants.

FEDERICO: Money's no object: do it tonight.

TRISTAN: A thousand crowns.

RICARDO: Done.

TRISTAN: Deposit?

RICARDO: Take this chain.

TRISTAN: Start counting the money.

FEDERICO: I'll go for it.

TRISTAN: I'll go for him.
Not a word: or we're all dead men.

RICARDO and FEDERICO leave. TEODORO enters.

TEODORO: I saw you talking to those...murderers.

TRISTAN: The biggest fools you could imagine.
They gave me this lovely gold chain
and promised me one thousand crowns,
to kill you today.

TEODORO: What's going on?
Every time I see you, I tremble.

TRISTAN: If only you'd heard me spouting Greek,
you'd have given me even more
than I got from those two idiots.
It's the easiest thing in the world.
Greekopolous speakopolou.
You make it up as you go along.

TEODORO: You've really dropped me in it this time.
They'll have my head if this comes out.

TRISTAN: Use your head and stop panicking.

TEODORO: You dig the holes, I stand in them.

TRISTAN: Just let things take their natural course.
They'll work out.

TEODORO: Diana's coming!

TRISTAN: Best she doesn't see me for now.

TRISTAN conceals himself just before DIANA enters.

DIANA: Aren't you going to see your father?

TEODORO: Something tragic has happened.
I've made my final decision:
I beg your leave to go to Spain.

DIANA: What's Marcela been saying this time?

TEODORO: Marcela? How could...?

DIANA: Then what is it?

TEODORO: It's not something that I can say.

DIANA: Tell me what it is; no matter
            how much it offends my honour.

TEODORO: Tristan, to whom Mischief should dedicate
            some verses, Deceit a statue,
            and Trickery should acknowledge
            as the undisputed master
            of its labyrinthine maze.
            Tristan, knowing how much I love you,
            seeing me in eternal despair,
            and learning of the Count's lost son,
            has created a fantasy
            of terrifying proportions.
            I have no father, no family,
            other than my wit, my books, my pen.
            Now the Count believes I'm his son.
            And although I could be your husband,
            and have more joy than I've dreamed of,
            I won't live with you in a lie.
            I won't sully your name, your blood
            or your house. That's why, my love,
            I have no choice but to go to Spain.

DIANA: You are both shrewd and foolish.
            Shrewd because you've demonstrated
            to me how noble you are,
            and foolish to take me for a fool.
            For a fool is what I would be
            if I said I'd not marry you.
            You may be just a commoner,
            but I've found the cover I needed,
            and perhaps some of the fire as well.
            Pleasure doesn't depend on rank

122

or station, but on the adjusting
of that which we desire to our needs.
I will marry you, rest assured.
But we must keep Tristan's mouth shut.
When he's asleep I'll have him drugged,
and they'll brick him up in the wall.

TRISTAN shouts from his hiding place.

TRISTAN: Walls have ears!

DIANA: Who's that?

TRISTAN: Me, Tristan,
who's shocked at the worst ingratitude
that any woman's ever shown.
Wall me up, when I've been a brick,
when I've moved both heaven and earth
for both of you.

DIANA: What did you hear?

TRISTAN: You're not turning me into stone.
I'm off.

DIANA: Wait.

TRISTAN: 'Wait', she says.

DIANA: Yes, wait.
If you promise you'll keep our secret,
then you'll find no better friend than me.

TRISTAN: Why would I not keep it a secret?
I have as much to lose as you.

TEODORO: What's that noise?

*Count LUDOVICO enters with CAMILO, accompanied by
FEDERICO, RICARDO, FABIO, ANARDA, DOROTEA and
MARCELA.*

RICARDO: We want to meet him!

FEDERICO: The whole of Naples is waiting
for him to appear at the door!

LUDOVICO: With Diana's permission,
Teodoro, there's a carriage waiting
to take you home, where you were born.
With a noble guard of honour,
as befits such an occasion.

DIANA: Sir, there is one thing you must know.
We are betrothed.

LUDOVICO: My darling girl,
you've made me the happiest of men.
Fortune's wheel should turn no further.
Stay it now with a golden nail.
I came for one child, and leave with two.

FEDERICO: Aren't you going to congratulate
my cousin, Ricardo?

RICARDO: Yes, but first
I must congratulate Teodoro,
on still being alive. Enraged
by jealousy, I hired this rogue
for the price of a golden chain
and a thousand crowns, to kill you.
I denounce him before you all.
Arrest him. He's a criminal.

TEODORO: Arrest him? For defending me?
For being loyal to his master?

RICARDO: For being loyal to his master?
He's a cut-throat, believe me.

TEODORO: No. He really is my servant.
And to reward this service
– and a number of other ones –
I give his hand to Dorotea.
And you Marcela'll marry Fabio,
as Diana's already decreed.

RICARDO: I offer to pay her dowry.

FEDERICO: I'll gladly pay Dorotea's.

LUDOVICO: Then all that remains is for me
to provide the final endowment;
my son and everything that's mine
will be yours, my sweetest daughter.

TEODORO: Then this is where it all should end,
when Fortune's wheel should cease her rolling.
But to all you who've watched our play,
I say this: keep our secret safe.
One slip, one forgetful moment,
and this secret comes tumbling out.

Printed in the USA
CPSIA information can be obtained
at www.ICGtesting.com
LVHW020844171024
794056LV00002B/388